NABLO

Competitiveness Through Total Cycle Time

Competitiveness Through Total Cycle Time

An Overview for CEOs

By **Philip R. Thomas**

With **Kenneth R. Martin**

McGraw-Hill Publishing Company

New York St. Louis San Francisco Auckland Bogotá
Caracas Hamburg Lisbon London Madrid Mexico
Milan Montreal New Delhi Oklahoma City
Paris San Juan São Paulo Singapore
Sydney Tokyo Toronto

Library of Congress Catalog Card Number: 89-29684

Total Cycle Time, Cycles of Learning, and The Five I's Process
are trademarks of Thomas Group, Inc.

234567890   DOC/DOC   96543210

ISBN 0-07-064273-7

*The editors for this book were James Bessent and Alfred Bernardi, the
designer was Naomi Auerbach, and the production supervisor was
Suzanne W. Babeuf. It was set in Baskerville by the McGraw-Hill
Publishing Company Professional & Reference Division composition
unit.*

Printed and bound by R. R. Donnelley & Sons Company.

*For more information about other McGraw-Hill materials,
call 1-800-2-MCGRAW in the United States. In other
countries, call your nearest McGraw-Hill office.*

To every person who shares in the endeavors of Thomas Group, Inc., and who strives to make businesses competitive—employees, associates, colleagues, friends, and family.

Contents

Preface

The Fast Can Out-Perform the Big

I first became interested in fast response in business in 1960 at age 25. After five years working in two large electronics companies, preceded by 2 years in the RAF and 3 years in the family business, it was my first shot at running a company. This first general management responsibility involved a small business of approximately 100 employees designing, manufacturing, and selling electronic equipment to the luxury yacht market. It was appropriately located in Southampton on the English Channel. It was in this setting that I developed the awareness of our ability to out-perform larger competitors by bringing new products to market very quickly and by responding far more rapidly to the many custom product requirements we received from our very demanding and sometimes fickle customers.

The Big Can Also Be Fast, and Out-Perform the Slow

A year later I crossed over into the semiconductor industry to work on integrated circuits. (They had only been invented in 1959.) Semiconductors turned out to be an extremely demanding business, with rapid growth and rapid product obsolescence, again, a business in which fast response could make the difference.

A stint at Texas Instruments followed, where as a general manager I was able to begin applying these concepts of cycle-time reduction. By the late sixties, I had applied the concept across the spectrum of business processes, from order entry, scheduling, planning, manufacturing, and shipping to the processes of product definition, design, and transfer to cost-effective manufacturing. This enabled my corner of the organization to out-perform its California competitor on shared custom contracts. Our response time through our total process was approximately one-fifth of our competitor's. Moreover, we constantly encouraged the customer to change desired shipping schedules to meet his exact needs, knowing we were the only supplier that could respond.

At this point, it became possible to establish many fundamental principles of Total Cycle Time and to gain first-hand experience of its many dramatic competitive advantages. I was also able to realize the significant improvements that resulted—in almost every aspect of the business—from creating a short-cycle-time culture.

Cycles of Learning Have More Leverage Than Volume

Subsequently, it became clear that classical experience curve theory, which predicts that the supplier with the largest market share will have the lowest cost and make the most profit, had a fundamental flaw. It overlooks the dramatic impact of short cycle time and the potential to exploit the resulting high number of Cycles of Learning, the opportunities to improve performance that occur when the lessons of experience are systematically exploited. The rate of change in cost, quality, and productivity are driven far more by the intelligent use of Cycles of Learning than by the cumulative volume of historical and present production.

Does It Work in Other Cultures?

Concerned that the impacts of short cycle time might be company culture dependent, I spent the next six years in three other companies with different locations and quite different cultures. In each case, on the East Coast, the West Coast, and the Midwest, in Europe and the Pacific Rim, the operations in which I applied TCT concepts and changed over to a short-cycle-time culture experienced radical improvements in performance.

The culture changes effected included a change in mindset, requiring people to think in terms of radical change instead of incremental changes, to consider how to make the giant leap from weeks of time to hours, not how to make incremental reductions to fewer weeks. By 1978, I was absolutely certain that the most powerful strategic and operational weapon was indeed time, and by this time had developed a detailed understanding and methods for establishing performance entitlement, the optimum performance level attainable by a business using existing resources, for dramatically reducing cycle times, and for exploiting Cycles of Learning to significantly accelerate results. Customers themselves considered the improved responsiveness to their requirements to be little short of spectacular. Internally, the businesses moved quickly to using far fewer resources and achieving very high productivity, particularly in the white-collar areas. Another benefit that had been surfacing in each situation over the prior 18 years was improved morale, which rose as the external and internal business processes improved.

Can It Be Done from the Sidelines?

Curious as to whether the successes could be repeated and whether the principles of TCT could be taught to and effectively utilized by CEOs and other top managers, I decided to go it on my own. I formed a company devoted to TCT exclusively and to helping other companies, especially manufacturing-based ones in North America (home now), to improve competitiveness worldwide by changing over to a short-cycle-time culture. The challenge has been getting top management to listen to such seemingly radical concepts and believe in the potential results. The reward is that now, eleven years later, the results speak for themselves.

It's Time to Get the Word Out

It is now clear that improved competitiveness through TCT is a reality and can be made to work in a wide range of corporate cultures and national cultures. The unique experiences described above, together with the needs of U.S. industry, has prompted me to write this book explaining to CEOs how TCT is applied and how it can drive improvements in competitiveness by improving responsiveness, accelerating results, and increasing resource effectiveness.

Locked up in practically every corporation are enough current resources to achieve levels of performance that are, in general, dramatically higher than current, or baseline, performance would indicate—with no change in layout, no automation, and rarely more software. I am confidently encouraging businesses to reach entitlement before automating. It is important to recognize that the big do not out-perform the little; the fast most frequently out-perform the slow.

In Appreciation

Many organizations and people have made it possible for me to develop these concepts, to apply them, to achieve measurable results, and many have contributed to my understanding through critique or feedback or by being part of the responsive organizations with which I have been fortunate enough to work. It is a tremendously exciting thing to see an organization turn around to a position of increased competitiveness. This is a feeling we all share at Thomas Group. We constantly learn from each other and are continuously improving and refining methods of accelerating the change to a competitive-response culture.

A Closing Thought

It is important to recognize that competitiveness through Total Cycle Time and the resulting responsiveness to customers' needs cannot be legislated, edicted, automated, or bought. It can only be managed by leadership that knows what it is doing. An overall approach to competitiveness through TCT can drive businesses rapidly ahead to entitled positions of world leadership in business.

PHILIP R. THOMAS

Foreword

The United States needs an awakening. Changes in expectation levels and in mind-set are needed. Our leaders must accept and inspire change throughout our culture if we are to be competitive in the global markets. The concept of entitlement performance is fundamental to achieving competitiveness in the global economy.

This forthright book maps a roadway to that goal. Very few companies are performing at their entitled level. However, if each company in the United States pursued its entitled performance with the right mind-set, the Gross National Product growth rate would increase substantially. There would be a sharp resurgence in this country's markets and a return to a positive balance of payments. But recapturing that competitive edge requires nothing less than fundamental cultural change.

The impact of cycle time was demonstrated to me in late 1971 when Phil Thomas toured me through his operations and showed me the superior results his team was obtaining.

Since that time, I have been sensitive to short-cycle-time performance, and I am frustrated by the waste associated with long cycle times.

To my knowledge, this book is the first complete approach to Total Cycle Time as a competitive tool. It is not theory or fables. It is based upon a wealth of experience gained from successfully applying the concepts to many businesses. *Competitiveness Through Total Cycle Time* focuses primarily on bringing awareness of the concepts and their potential impacts to top executives of manufacturing-based industry. It is written in the manner of a parable.

I believe the concepts should be broadly applied to service industries, military, government, and the education field. Let me make the point with an extreme example: These management skills applied to the defense procurement problem should cut the Total Cycle Time in that area in half. Total Cycle Time is the total elapsed time from the recognition of a need to fulfilling that need, be the need a new tank, a new helicopter, or whatever. In some areas of the Armed Forces, Total Cycle Time runs almost 20 years!

Reduction of the Department of Defense's Total Cycle Time should allow the United States to have the most modern armed forces in the world at *half* the current $300 billion budget. This would allow the United States to be the strongest nation in the world (lowest cost, most modern, and most effective), *without* overloading its economy with large DOD expenditures.

If we applied these approaches in every area of our economy to eliminate nonvalue-added costs, raise quality, improve productivity, and shorten the time to availability of new products, services, weapon systems, and education, our global position would be enhanced dramatically.

Competitiveness Through Total Cycle Time reveals insights shared with top executives in many companies over the last ten years. Based on my prior experiences with these concepts, I know that Total Cycle Time works. As you read, you will begin to see ways to use Total Cycle Time in your endeavors. That is as it should be, because you cannot resist the energy—and the urgency—of Philip Thomas's message. Total Cycle Time is a message that must be heard.

> J. FRED BUCY*
> *Retired President*
> *Texas Instruments, Incorporated*

---

*During his career at Texas Instruments, Mr. Bucy was head of the Defense Systems Group from 1963 to 1967, head of the Semiconductor Group from 1967 to 1972, Executive Vice President from 1972 to 1976, and President of the company from 1976 until his retirement in 1985. He now takes on individual projects he believes important to improving U.S. competitiveness at the state and national levels.

1
Challenge

Times are changing for business. The technological revolution has freed human creativity. Volume of trade is accelerating dramatically in an atmosphere of intense competition. Time has become the crucial factor in business survival. As product lifetimes shorten and variety increases, there are opportunities galore; but disaster awaits any company that lacks quick market response.

This book will demonstrate that a company's strategy for survival and success must be based upon a culture of competitive performance that I call Total Cycle Time. Total Cycle Time is the time it takes from the expression of a customer's need until that need is satisfied. Within that period lie a multitude of discrete activities, each with its own cycle time. Total Cycle Time culture identifies every one of those cycles, blue-collar and white-collar, and shortens them by eliminating unnecessary obstacles to productivity.

Shortening cycle times is a matter of systematically removing barriers and constantly using the feedback of ongoing experience to streamline the task at hand. A Total Cycle Time company works better, not harder, or longer, or faster, or at reduced quality. Its managers have learned to regard business as a seamless process instead of a series of disjointed functions, and to operate accordingly.

Adopting such a culture—and making it permanent—enables a company to reduce the time it takes to develop and manufacture a product, deliver a service, enter an order, install a factory, procure materials, and improve quality while cutting costs. Total Cycle Time is not a miracle cure from Asia or a how-to recipe from the latest industrial guru, but the product of twenty-four years of trial and refinement. It works. Furthermore, it works in virtually every type of business.

If you are an attentive businessperson, you are probably familiar with cycle time theory, at least in the manufacturing realm. No doubt you also appreciate that time to market is a critical element in competitiveness. Few people, however, understand the profound relationship of cycle time to overall performance, which is why the following situations may prove interesting or even surprising. As you read them, please note that, conventional wisdom to the contrary, the causes of the problems are rooted in cycle times.

Do some of these predicaments sound familiar?

* * *

Imagine yourself manager of a business whose newest product came onto the market late and lacks the attractive features by which your competition's product has grabbed market share. This fiasco has come in the wake of your marketing people's expressed fear that the new item might be lackluster, and despite an endless series of product reviews that proved unable to correct the problem. To prevent future foul-ups of this sort, you consider spending more on market research and implementing more exacting project review processes.

Will such steps, you wonder, prevent future damage? You are sure that your market research team is competent, hampered only by its inability to project far into the future. Yet your happy competitors seem to have surmounted this problem. Was your project review system perhaps not rigorous enough? Unlikely, you decide, inasmuch as the product's design was repeatedly fine-tuned during development. If it had been any more rigorous, the new item would still be waiting in the wings.

Coming to the market too late with too little cannot be remedied by adding steps to the developmental process. More market research bespeaks a need to see *too* far into the future because your development takes too long. Likewise, adding more steps to the design review process will cause counterproductive delays. The root of your problem is the fact that your company couldn't respond to a market opportunity in timely fashion. You are going to have to cut cycle times dramatically. Later in this book, I will explain how.

*   *   *

As a well-meaning CEO, you find you are up to your eyeballs in complaints. Increasingly dissatisfied customers are calling you directly instead of going through channels, so you hear first-hand that your company's on-time delivery performance has dropped by half. Your customers have learned that a call to you will expedite matters, and it is costing your company a fortune to rush orders through on your command.

What is wrong here? Marketing seems unable to forecast far enough ahead for manufacturing to respond to customer needs. Your marketing director says the problem is the customers: they are requesting products on shorter and shorter notice and are changing their minds more and more often after entering orders. These new developments are raising havoc within the company, creating a vicious circle of pressure, failure, complaints, and emergencies.

Would a more elaborate management information system help managers get product out the door on time? That is doubtful. As your manufacturing manager puts it, more data to more people might simply cause more mismanagement. He reminds you that his actual two-week manufacturing time is quite short—once he knows what he is supposed to be making—but it takes longer to enter a customer's order than it does to manufacture it. And because the planning cycle occurs monthly, there are frequent shortages and outages.

In this case, the crux of the problem is that the manufacturing and marketing cycle times far exceed the real market visibility. As a result, work-in-process inventories build up. In addition, the long cycle time reduces predictability of output. Some products are completed in short order; others seem to take forever, which is why you've been getting those irate calls. Your own conscientious efforts to expedite lagging orders are causing further confusion on the manufacturing floor.

You had better forget the notion of increasing the management information system your people have to work with, and stop nagging your marketers for better forecasts. Concentrate instead on reducing the cycle time of each step in the manufacturing and marketing process.

* * *

Your company suddenly identifies a strategic opportunity that will necessitate 30 percent growth over the next year. You are ready to take the plunge, but your hopes are dashed when your comptroller itemizes the financial requirements for such a move. The comptroller reports that you will need more cash than you have on hand, and your lines of credit are already stretched. All you can do is pull in your horns and settle for less. Never again! you promise yourself.

The next time such a growth opportunity appears, you can have a clear shot at it if you apply the concepts of Total Cycle Time. Any company, regardless of its size or the nature of its business, should be able to liberate enough funds to support a 30 percent growth surge because, measurably and predictably, Total Cycle Time reduces the need to tie up cash, liberating funds for growth opportunities.

* * *

You and your company have been struggling for five years to improve quality. As CEO, you've attended seminars, you've installed the "right" training programs, and you've put in all sorts of controls. But you're still frustrated by the slow progress of your program, which is being outdistanced by competitors' quality improvement.

Are your controls inadequate? Probably not. In fact, you probably have too many. Is it too easy for people to change procedures to suit themselves? Should more sign-offs be inserted to control that tendency? Again, probably not. It is likely that you already have too many signature requirements in your sign-off loop. Finally, are your quality measurements adequate? Like most, they may be adequate in terms of absolute standards but inadequate in terms of fundamental control.

The frustrations and uncertainties you feel are common to thousands of quality programs in every corner of U.S. industry. Such programs are stirring testimony to the nation's reemphasis on high quality; but, too often, they go haywire because they are treated as programs and are not integrated into the corporate culture. Moreover, they are often at cross purposes to their goal because they lengthen cycle times. Believe it or not—and I intend to make you a believer—long, painstaking cycle times actually reduce quality; short cycle times improve it. The surest way to total quality improvement is a Total Cycle Time effort combined with a focus on quality.

* * *

You are determined to stop the erosion of your company's market share. Accordingly, your marketing director, who has carefully analyzed the market and your competitors' product offerings, has convinced you that over the next two years, your company must double the number of products it brings to the market.

How can you accomplish this miracle? You could double your development budget and hire twice as many development people, provided you had the money to do so, which you don't. You could zero in on the part of the market your company is best at, eliminate the rest, and become a highly specialized niche supplier. No good, says Marketing. In the long run, retreating to a niche will reduce your company's market share, competitive position, and profitability.

Or you could reduce cycle time. Cutting the cycle times of design and development by half or better will double the productivity of your research and development dollars and open larger windows of opportunity in the market. And if you have any doubts whatever about doubling productivity in white-collar bailiwicks such as design and development (or anywhere else), read on. You are in for some good news.

* * *

Everyone in your company has caught the competitive spirit. Your engineering manager recommends that the next machine your company purchases be the largest available, one with a humongous load size, so you can exploit economy of scale. Your marketing people, however, are jittery about such a move, saying they will have difficulty placing such large run sizes in the marketplace. Engineering's boss, your operations manager, argues that the dilemma might be eased if you would also authorize a better data package. More information, he suggests, will improve Marketing's forecasts and Manufacturing's response to the marketplace.

Here is a classic cycle time issue. In almost every business there is a tendency to move to larger machines that are presumed to be more cost-effective. Resist the urge to climb on the bandwagon. Go for the alternative: shorten your manufacturing cycle time by using smaller machines and smaller run sizes that are optimized for the marketplace instead of the capacity of a mechanical colossus.

* * *

You own an advertising business that sidelines in promotional literature. Your costs and turnaround time for customers is average for the industry. Just when you are feeling comfortable, you start losing business to a competitor no larger than yourself who delivers in far less time and at lower cost than you can achieve. To make matters worse, your customers tell you pointedly that this competitor's quality is tops. You get the message.

You find out as much as you can from your wavering customers and listen carefully to the grapevine. Your rival's data systems and equipment are much like your own; even the caliber of her employees looks about the same. What, then, is her secret weapon?

You are head to head with someone who has shortened cycle time. While you were holding your own at the accepted performance level for the industry—a level I call baseline—your competitor had realized the actual performance capability of his business—a level I call entitlement. Although entitlement performance requires no more resources than baseline, the difference between the two is often astonishing. Your competitor will be snatching clients as long as you allow yourself the luxury of your accustomed cycle times.

Are You Entitled?

Most failures in performance and/or competitiveness are due to excessive cycle time. If this notion arouses skepticism, it is not surprising. Most businesspeople believe they are operating at or near their entitled performance level when, in truth, they are far below that. What is missing is Total Cycle Time culture. At the risk of straining your credibility further, it should be added that the nation's worldwide competitiveness crisis can be reversed if American companies will move from their accustomed baseline performance levels to their entitlement level. This can be accomplished without the addition of any new resources. What they must add is the culture of Total Cycle Time.

The chapters that follow outline the theory, practice, and institutionalization of the Total Cycle Time system and get down to cases that quantify its impact. In other words, they discuss not only what ought to be done but specifically how to do it.

Total Cycle Time is easy to grasp philosophically but, as will be demonstrated, difficult to implement. It is not a quick fix; but it is a breakthrough. It clears away obstacles, raises quality, improves asset utilization and customer service, and shortens time to market. It makes businesses very, very competitive.

Competition, Quality, and the Three R's

The United States is at last beginning to take the problems of international competitiveness seriously. Lately, improved performance in both the public and private sectors has become a formal national objective. During his inaugural speech in January 1989, President Bush departed from his prepared text to express concern over the competitiveness crisis. In doing so, he reiterated a position often expressed by his predecessor. Indeed, the federal government has for several years been discussing national programs to revitalize U.S. competitiveness; but time is slipping away.

Meanwhile, business leaders, statespersons, economists, and academicians, united by a sense of urgency and common purpose, are no longer satisfied to hope for the best, or to put their faith in the nation's knack for innovation, or to settle for short-run palliatives. Overcoming the competitiveness gap is obviously going to require a major renovation of business practices from coast to coast: a nationwide culture change.

Getting America competitive is a matter of displacing imports with domestic products and increasing exports by earning the respect of buyers at home and abroad. That means better products, faster. The United States will be competitive when the world prefers our products to those of other nations because American means superior features, quality, price, and timely availability.

There are three components of competitiveness, the Three R's, so to speak: responsiveness, results acceleration, and resource effectiveness. They are complementary, even symbiotic. The first, responsiveness, involves delivering what the consumer wants faster than the competition and with less inventory. That is accomplished through shortened cycle times. Responsive businesses enjoy an important advantage: namely, increased opportunities to learn from the feedback of experience, which I call Cycles of Learning. Conscientious use of such feedback will, in turn, accelerate results, with positive impact on market share, profit, return on assets, and quality, even as costs decline. Of course, as cycle times are reduced further, the use of resources—people, plant, equipment, inventory, and cash—increases in effectiveness.

One of the most gratifying steps in the struggle to improve competitiveness has been the realization by many companies that quality improvement is an ongoing strategic necessity, not just a nice idea. Better late than never. Although the connection between quality improvement and profitability has been well established for years, American companies have hesitated until lately to adopt that strategy, partly because their measurements and controls were geared to other criteria. Now that that has changed, corporatewide total quality strategies, designed to institutionalize quality improvement as an ongoing managerial responsibility, are finding favor throughout industry.

Total quality came into its own largely because American companies were getting clobbered by foreign competitors, notably Japanese, who offered superior goods and lower prices. To fight back, such companies have made a concerted effort to upgrade the quality of their own products. The results have been mixed.

Programs that stop short of a total approach are foredoomed because they fail to institutionalize higher quality into the corporate culture. Traditional measurements and controls remain in place; these can be manipulated to distort quality results. Even total quality efforts, however, often run aground because they fail to shorten business cycle times. In fact, they often do the opposite, with calamitous results. Characteristically, American quality programs add steps to the production process, which lengthens cycle times. This is especially true in the white-collar area, where paperwork increases as quality preoccupations rise. It is only by shortening cycle times that a quality program can get enough feedback from its Cycles of Learning to make necessary process improvements and eliminate unnecessary barriers. Total Cycle Time drives total quality.

Shorter cycle times are hard to sell to quality managers seeking to emulate Japanese methods. The Japanese maintain high quality by adding laborious steps to the production process; so anyone competing with them is inclined to do the same. Aping Japanese methods is a very dangerous game for an American company, however. Contrary to their well-managed publicity, the Japanese are poor asset managers. Their celebrated low-inventory "just in time" technique is more apparent than real. Most important, they do not appreciate cycle time thinking, and their unique societal culture predisposes them to painstaking, complicated quality control. Japanese managers are formidable data gatherers and analyzers but they are largely uncomfortable with rapid spontaneous decision making. Unlike Americans, whose historic pragmatism and receptivity to novel approaches make them shoo-ins for new methods, the Japanese are poor candidates for Total Cycle Time culture. They can be outmaneuvered in market after market if Americans will use Total Cycle Time to propel total quality.

The competitiveness crisis of the 1980s and 1990s is, of course, more than a matter of improving business performance and quality. Shortened cycle times can hasten earthshaking breakthroughs in other areas of endeavor. Consider advanced research aimed at conquering AIDS, for example. Conventional wisdom has it that basic research cannot be accelerated. However, if the research process can be defined and analyzed as a business process, and if the wasted, nonproductive time can be identified and eliminated, the overall process will be faster and more productive. Any concept that can substantially reduce the time necessary to develop an AIDS vaccine and/or can substantially reduce the cost thereof should receive immediate consideration.

Now consider aerospace and weapons systems. Such systems can be readied for production in a fraction of the time usually required. Thomas Group recently analyzed the effort required to manufacture a space satellite. Excluding design and development, the process currently runs almost three and one-half years. That time, it was determined, could be reduced to fifteen months. Inasmuch as every day of cycle time is worth about $100,000, such a reduction is decidedly nontrivial.

In weapons systems, Total Cycle Time packs a series of wallops that have global importance. Weapons development and manufacture is notoriously, sometimes scandalously, expensive and time-consuming. Decades of cost-plus defense contracting and the U.S. government's lavish resource allocation for the most finicky details have produced massive overhead, overstaffing, and a colossal waste of talent that is sorely needed elsewhere in American industry. Defense development cycles are so long that by the time they reach the field, "new" weapons often utilize obsolete technology. That, to put it mildly, is poor defense strategy. Five to fifteen years is too long a cycle for almost any business, defense or otherwise, in an age of rapid technological change. When it comes to weapons systems, cutting cycle times is a matter of national security.

Because Total Cycle Time's pertinence transcends the nation's business sector, it should be applied across the board in the federal and local governments to eliminate waste and reduce costs. Given the sometimes desperate measures presently being undertaken in the name of balancing the federal budget, that kind of strategy is long overdue; and think of the bite that such a bureaucratic culture change would take out of the current national deficit. To that end, I am working on a data system that will track the present administration and identify the most pressing gaps between baseline and entitlement performance therein.

Meanwhile, there is a great deal of talk around Washington about restoring the eroding work ethic and rekindling a sense of economic vitality in all citizens. If Washington is serious, a directed, nationwide effort to impart cycle time training is in order. Accordingly, academic institutions should move to include cycle time training as part of their business curricula.

The general institutionalization of Total Cycle Time thinking would have a profound economic effect. Within a few years' time, Total Cycle Time typically doubles a company's return on assets, substantially increases productivity, and cuts product development time in half. On a national scale, such improvements would radically alter the dynamics of money. The first major nation to accomplish this would possess a colossal advantage in international competitiveness: funding for direct research will have twice its previous effect, and new products will be brought to market in half the time (or less, if research is taken into account). In such a circumstance, the value generated per capita would skyrocket, with proportionate improvement in the national standard of living. It would also formidably position the United States for the world playoffs in military and aerospace technology, satellite utilization and telecommunications, and automation.

Is this a pipe dream? Not really. Senior managers from more than fifty companies in the United States and Europe have received previews of Total Cycle Time's capabilities. Their response has been enthusiastic. Managers, especially those who have been trying methods that come out of Asia, say that they are frustrated with their inability to effect culture change. They instantly grasp the gist of these new methods, and they see the possible impact on quality, customer response, accelerated results, and resource effectiveness.

Of course, the gist is easy to grasp; it is the doing that takes effort. And, in the competitiveness crisis, no one should confuse understanding, resolution, and dedication with action and results, for competitiveness cannot be legislated. It cannot be bought. It cannot be edicted by presidents, CEOs, or bureaucracies. It must be *managed*. In the final analysis, American managers must overcome the competitiveness gap by seeing to it that the nation delivers to the marketplace better, more reliable, more attractive products faster than anyone else. There is no other route to long-term competitiveness.

More than ever, companies are ready and eager to make that effort. One way or another, the next few years will be very, very exciting ones for Americans in general and American businesspeople in particular.

Admittedly, the recommendations of this chapter are sweeping generalizations that would require books to do them justice. I intend to write such books. I am also at work on a competitiveness index, a set of measurements and a test through which any company can quickly get some notion of its baseline and entitlement. When businesspeople can determine that gap, however tentatively, some of the initial psychological barriers to action may be eliminated.

Total Cycle Time

Originally, the first word of Total Cycle Time was intended to express how short cycle times can be applied productively to *all* segments of a business, not just manufacturing efforts. Already, however, the word *total* has expanded in importance to encompass several meanings. It still represents the fact that in the move from baseline to entitlement performance, short cycle times pervade every nook and cranny of an organization at every level. But, by fortuitous accident, it has also become associated with comprehensive programs for improving the quality of American products: total quality programs. The similarity of the two terms is very pleasing because Total Cycle Time fits hand in glove with quality throughout any business.

The word *total* is furthermore a reminder that short cycle time culture is applicable to all kinds of businesses: manufacturing, service, or otherwise. Finally, *total* suggests that the concept has transcendent possibilities. It can extend beyond the limits of commerce. Its message should—and will, I think—embrace scientific, academic, governmental, and military institutions.

In the eighties, Total Cycle Time has provided a major opportunity for businesses large and small to improve performance dramatically. But the playing field for business gets flatter and the market windows narrower. In the nineties, Total Cycle Time will become nothing less than a recipe for survival. In that context, it will not be the big that outperform the little, it will be the fast that out-perform the slow.

And Now for Our Story

It remains to demonstrate the nuts and bolts of Total Cycle Time. Selections from my company's backlog of case histories would do the trick, except for the issue of strict confidentiality with clients. That being the case, we have had to create a fictional company, General Widget Corp., as a vehicle.

Chapters 2 through 6 constitute a scenario in which General Widget endeavors to move from its baseline performance to its entitlement via Total Cycle Time. The sequence of events is, of course, fictional as are all the characters except myself. The scenario, however, represents a synthesis of many experiences deploying Total Cycle Time. Make no mistake: the elements of the story are fictionalized composites of specific situations encountered on dozens of occasions. Not a single incident in the scenario is totally fictionalized. All of the personal anecdotes are factual, whether or not the companies described are identified.

Care has been taken not to overdramatize the story. Accordingly, the timing and results described are typical, not exceptional, well within the range of our actual experience. What follows, therefore, is a generic rather than an extreme case of the adoption of Total Cycle Time. I believe you will find it readable, informative, and, hopefully, important.

2
Action

Thomas Group's involvement with the widget business began with the appearance of an article in a major national weekly magazine outlining the woes of that industry and its uncertainty about how to cope with overseas competition. The story was the familiar one of established companies losing market share to new Japanese competitors. On the strength of that article, we had sent videotape cassettes describing Total Cycle Time to the presidents of several American widget firms.

A month after the mailing, I received a telephone call at our home office from Victor King, president and chairman of General Widget Corp. We talked for about twenty minutes.

King first confirmed the substance of the magazine article, but before getting down to specifics, he ran me through the expected identity questions. I assured him that we were implementers experienced at improving performance in industry and that there was not a single person on my payroll from the consulting industry. King remained a bit leery because, as he put it, "In the past few years we have had several consultants here trying without much success to figure out why our business is stagnating and our market share is dropping. We do more than half a billion in annual business.

We're still profitable and we have quite a few of our indices under control. We've got good people around here, but we can't seem to fight off this Japanese threat, despite the expensive advice we've been getting. We've taken a lot of that advice but haven't been able to really make headway. I'm close enough to other firms in the business to know that the problem is foreign, not domestic, competition. We've been operating more than sixty years, and the company enjoys considerable loyalty on the part of workers. Around here, we don't use the word *culture*, but our esprit de corps is very real, although it has taken a beating lately. We like to think that over the years we've been doing things right, and the consensus of top management is that if it ain't broke, you shouldn't fix it. Well, it ain't broke, exactly, but we sure as hell have got to do something different if we're going to survive.

"The Japanese—newcomers, you know—are outmaneuvering us. Fifteen years ago, they scarcely knew what a widget was. Now, several companies over there are turning out widgets loaded with innovative features. Just last year they introduced a self-adjusting, nonskid model that was priced slightly cheaper than the conventional design we're all used to. Confidentially, their quality is better than ours, and we're no slouches. We own a subsidiary assembly plant on Taiwan. Given the deterioration of our position, I'm under pressure to relocate more of the business there; but my financial VP says that could cause more problems than it would solve. By now, you can probably see why I called you."

I could. As he talked further, I could also see that King had digested our videotape and had picked up on one of its crucial points: that Total Cycle Time involves a fundamental overhaul of baseline practices and the permanent adoption of new attitudes, methods, measurements, and controls; many months of effort, all in all. Accordingly, he needed reassurance that our people would work on site through all phases of the move to entitlement, and was intrigued when I told him we would be glad to work on an incentive basis.

But it was too soon to come to the point of negotiating, so he resumed his introductory description: "One of our two biggest problems is our difficulty in responding to customer requirements. It's not as if we're on a technological roller-coaster. General Widget's products usually have an eight-year life. But despite that, we're hard put to meet our customers' demand for faster changes in the mix of products we ship. In this area, Japanese competitors can dance rings around us because they apparently keep enough inventory on hand to ship in whatever mix they're asked for. Frankly, we don't have the cash to do that.

"Our other problem is new products. I would guess that a third of our sales are from products introduced within the last three years. I see the significance of that and so does our design team. We're always at work on new items with features that, we're sure, can't fail in the market, but it takes us so long to get them to market that the Japanese have usually arrived there ahead of us. There's a lot of frustration in this company right now."

I said it looked to me as though General Widget's problems ranged from design and development through manufacturing and marketing. I suggested that we might do a brief preliminary assessment of baseline and entitlement for those sectors of the company.

"Our team won't distract your organization for long," I told King. "With your cooperation, we can probably accomplish our data gathering in less than two weeks. We'll extract the information we need about your costs, yields, productivity, utilization of capacity, and inventories, interview key people, and bring the data back to headquarters for analysis. That will permit us to assess baseline and entitlement and estimate entitlement's impact on your overall business effectiveness. Then you can decide whether or not to proceed, with or without us."

But King was reeling me in slowly. He changed the subject to one that obviously had caused him considerable perplexity at General Widget. He had been with the company since the

fifties, he said, and had watched its white-collar payroll over-
take and exceed that of the direct-labor force. Putting that
fact together with some of my impact statements on the videotape, he had concluded that Total Cycle Time might be a
good investment. I reassured him that the impact figures we
cited were not casual, and that a 25 percent increase in white-
collar productivity was a reasonable expectation.

His rejoinder, however, was shrewd: "If you can increase
white-collar performance levels that much, what do I do with
all the surplus people?" That, I told him, depended upon the
amount of market potential in his business. By the sound of
his remarks, it was obvious that the problem was not the market, but General Widget's share of it.

After briefly discussing the incentive basis for our services,
King requested an outline of the statement of work, with
résumés of the key people who would be working on this initial project. The particulars were faxed to him, and within a
few days, he called to say he had decided to proceed with a
preliminary assessment. We set a date to make a presentation
to him and his key subordinates in Philadelphia six weeks
hence. While waiting for the preparatory information packet
he agreed to send, I ordered a Dun & Bradstreet report on
General Widget and had my assistant root around in the clipping files.

We always start our business day early, but when a new client is identified, I like to get to the office at the crack of dawn
and go over the new material. There, in the almost spooky
silence of the twenty-fifth floor, as the early bright begins to
suffuse the room, I can concentrate without distraction. That
was the scene when I began to study up on General Widget.
I had been provided with several articles covering the company and the business in general. They told me that General
Widget had begun life in the early twenties, when its
founder, the late Robert "Cap'n Bob" Martin, a celebrated
World War I ace, began turning out custom-designed widgets from his Philadelphia garage. The company flourished
as a family enterprise, propelled by the consumer boom of

the twenties. By 1927, when it went public, General Widget had a foot in both the industrial and consumer markets, supplying widgets to end users in the automotive, appliance, and apparel businesses, with small sidelines in hobby shops and hardware stores. It had just completed construction of a plant and office building in North Philadelphia when Black Friday occurred.

General Widget made it through the great depression rather well by trimming its consumer line and relying on the indispensability of its industrial models to see it through. With a work force of almost five hundred, the company never missed a payroll, a fact that made "Cap'n Bob" a hero to his employees and laid the cornerstone for a family-style culture that not even unionization in the forties could kill off. Meanwhile, gathering war clouds produced new opportunities to exploit electromechanical and nylon-reinforced improvements for military purposes. Even before Pearl Harbor, the company was expanding dramatically, supplying America's rapid arms buildup and beleaguered Britain's needs. By the time the United States entered World War II, a pair of three-story, brick, functionally modern plants had been completed adjacent to the original building. By the end of hostilities, the work force, too, had risen to more than eight thousand.

While not exactly a household name, General Widget, like many other firms, skillfully exploited wartime advertising to keep its name before the public ("General Widget Leads The Charge!" "Widget-backed P-38s Hit The Axis Where It Hurts!"). More important, concurrent advances in electronics, plastics, and "Day-glo" paints improved both the quality and versatility of the product line, placing the company in an ideal position to exploit the postwar consumer bonanza.

In the fifties and sixties, General Widget cultivated a balance between defense contracting, industrial business, and consumer goods. Changing technology, however, reduced the Pentagon's reliance upon widgetry, and by the latter seventies, the company's military contracting had declined to a small but consistent 20 percent of annual sales. Hopes for retail consumer sales had proven similarly disappointing. Sponsorship of arty TV programs and a saturation advertising campaign featuring "Widgie," a perky homemaker whose "widget wisdom" had rewarded her with a sparkling house and doting family, could not offset the product's drawbacks of short shelf life and a poor service network. Accordingly, General Widget's retail business stayed small, averaging only 10 percent of annual sales through the seventies and eighties. Industrial markets, however, proved to be another story. Identified in 1955 as the company's bread and butter by then Vice President King, industrial applications had mushroomed, more than compensating for the decline in defense contracting.

By the eighties, General Widget enjoyed longstanding relationships with corporate giants, thanks to its consistent quality and economy of scale, if not innovativeness. But times were changing for widget makers, who for too long had relied upon established markets and mature technology to see them through. And it must have been galling to see still another classic American invention co-opted, improved, and built cheaper by foreigners. King's remark to me on the telephone a few days earlier had been on the money: General Widget sure as hell had to do something different if it was going to survive. Here was a challenge.

By the time I had finished my preliminary study, the office had livened up and a secretary delivered to my desk the requested data package from Philadelphia. Its contents revealed that General Widget had done about $600 million in sales during the last fiscal year, a substantial sum but no improvement over the three preceding years. The company employed 6500 people. Total assets were $400 million; return on assets was 4.5 percent; visible inventory amounted to $95 million. Revenue per person was $92.5 thousand—not bad. Employee turnover was small. Pretax profit, however, was only 5 percent: $30 million, and the company was paying a tax rate of 40 percent. The company was functionally organized, served by four vice presidents (Research and Development, Marketing, Operations, and Finance) and a quality director, all of whom reported directly to King, and all of whom would be key players in General Widget's move to entitlement.

I shared the information with the four team members scheduled to go with me to Philadelphia.

Personalities

We were met at our hotel near Philadelphia International Airport by a General Widget driver and a very large and shiny black Chrysler. The ride to the company site seemed to take forever, but it was still early morning when we pulled up before the Art Deco building "Cap'n Bob" had built in the late twenties, a structure whose ornate flourishes were, alas, a thing of the past. In the reception area, beneath a faintly smiling portrait of the founder, a polished object about the size of a cantaloupe, ensconced like a piece of fine sculpture on a rotating pedestal, caught my eye. It was a rare example of General Widget's first product.

Buzzed by the receptionist, Victor King emerged: tweedy, graying, and different than I had expected. Firm handshakes were given all around; then King ushered us into a paneled conference room whose only decor was a series of framed photographs of vintage aircraft, cars, and kitchens, all presumably widgetized. A screen and overhead projector had been provided for my introductory talk. Now began the inspiration phase of Total Cycle Time.

First impressions: several people, seated at the conference table, broke off their subdued conversations in midsyllable and rose the instant King entered. All had been advised about the purpose and potential importance of the meeting. One by one, they introduced themselves as we gathered by a sideboard loaded with coffee cups and pastries.

Vice President of Finance Prudence Cash, stylish and

fortyish, had been with the company ten years, three in her present job. I judged from the attentiveness others gave to her introductory pleasantries that she commanded peer respect.

Hardy Sellers, Vice President of Marketing, might have been sent by Central Casting. A gladhanding, prepossessing, 6-foot extrovert in his early fifties, he possessed the requisite affability, booming voice, and tailored suit that were tools of his trade. Was there substance beneath the style?

Dr. Witt Tinker, Vice President of Research and Development, was fairly new to the company, and appeared less at ease than the others. Despite his beard, he looked to be the youngest member of the group by at least a decade, and enough emphasis had been placed upon the title preceding his name to indicate that his academic achievement was important to him. Although all the males present had arrived in jacket and tie, Tinker was the only one not wearing a white shirt.

Haggard Prince, Vice President of Operations, had been with General Widget more than twenty years, during which he worked himself up through the ranks of manufacturing and served for awhile in the planning function. He had been in his current job for five years, which meant he was feeling the pinch of the company's recent stagnation. That may have accounted for the bags under his eyes and the touch of middle age spread that tugged at the button of his suit coat. He reminded me of a lot of other senior executives I'd met who had reached the make-or-break point in their careers. Prince was undoubtedly a man beset by distractions. Did he possibly fear that these strangers from Dallas were going to distract him further?

Prince had three of his four immediate subordinates in tow. (The fourth, who managed General Widget's plant at Kaohsiung, Taiwan, was absent for obvious reasons.) All were in their fifties; none appeared to be enjoying themselves. L. J. Byer, Purchasing Manager, was too shy to be sized up at all. Eve Proctor, Production Control Manager, was another long-time employee who had risen through the clerical ranks. During our group chat she was kidded, not too gently, about her punctiliousness. She obviously had no idea what she was doing at this meeting.

Neither did Percy "Butch" McMills, Manufacturing Manager—or so he said. McMills was one of a vanishing breed of hard knocks managers. He was built like a fireplug. He had a pencil behind his ear and had already doffed his coat. His crew cut and a forearm tattoo ("SEMPER FIDELIS"), visible below the short sleeve of his shirt, spoke volumes, but he did his own talking.

"We've all seen your tape," he told me, "and I've been prepped for this meeting, but I don't know why we're here. General Widget's doing okay. We're comparable to the other people in the industry. I'm sure of that because I know most of the other people."

A similar sentiment was registered by Hunter Meritt, Quality Control Manager. I had read that Meritt was a one-time contender who had been edged out by Prince for the operations vice presidency. As quality manager, he reported directly to King, an arrangement General Widget's customers' had insisted upon after several expensive quality glitches. Meritt seemed dead serious about quality and demonstrably proud of the company's improving record in that area.

As a group, General Widget's top managers appeared competent but hardly charismatic. They displayed mutual respect and were comfortable with each other, although heads turned in unison whenever King spoke. There were enough humorous asides to indicate that all were well acquainted, but I doubted their friendships went beyond the workplace. In any event, this was the group that would make or break Total Cycle Time if General Widget opted to change its culture.

Inspiration

It was time for my introductory presentation. First came the matter of credibility. I began with a list of the heavyweight corporations we had helped in ten years of our existence. I

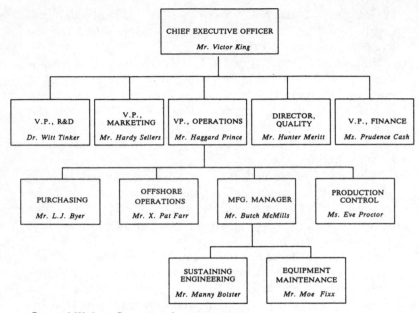

General Widget Company, key management.

identified myself as a former executive in the semiconductor business who had risen through the managerial ranks at Texas Instruments, General Instrument, Fairchild, and RCA. During those years, I had perfected the concept of Total Cycle Time and had successfully deployed it in very different corporate cultures. Since 1979, I told my audience, I and my colleagues had installed Total Cycle Time in dozens of companies, every one a success story. General Widget, I assured them, would be no exception.

Then came the inspirational part of the presentation. Practice had allowed me to trim such remarks to the bare essentials because the impact of the message can overwhelm unprepared listeners. To move things along, I had brought a stack of transparent foils to use with an overhead projector, and had also equipped every attendee with a packet of visual aids.

Cycle Times, Actual versus Theoretical

I explained the concept of baseline versus entitlement performance, stressing that almost every company operates at the former while imagining itself at the latter, although the gap between the two is usually very large.

"We want to determine those two reference points at General Widget," I explained. "Experience has taught me that the key measurement of performance is cycle time: the elapsed time between the start and completion of an operation. In manufacturing, it can be calculated as the number of units of work-in-process inventory divided by the number of units processed in a specific time period. If, for example, a manufacturing line has work-in-process inventory of 400 units and can process 100 units a day, its

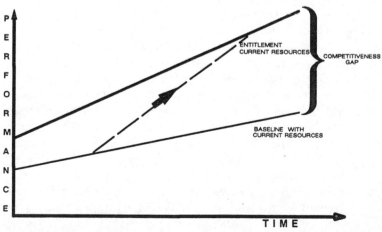

Competitiveness gap.

cycle time is four days. But cycle time thinking goes far beyond mere manufacturing, so here's a different example: If a company has 100 orders in process and is entering orders at the rate of 50 a week, its order-entry-cycle time is two weeks." I saw McMills and Prince nod knowingly. Tinker and Cash were starting to take notes. King just fixed me with an unwavering gaze.

I pressed on: "My long love affair with cycle times began as a line manager in the semiconductor industry. I really believe that it was the superheated environment of that industry that inspired me to look at cycle times analytically. It was and is the curse of the semiconductor business to suffer long, agonizing design and manufacturing problems in bringing to market products whose commercial life span is quite short. Because speed and precision are the roads to commercial success, the pressure to eliminate design and manufacturing roadblocks is intense.

"Despite that pressure, as a semiconductor manager I had never encountered an operation that wasn't capable of using its resources more effectively than its present performance indicated. The problem for me always was to determine what the possible (entitlement) performance level might be. For a long time, I used common sense. Then I hit upon the idea of theoretical cycle time.

"Theoretical cycle time is the back-to-back process time required for a single unit to complete all stages of a task without waiting, stoppage, or setups. Once I computed theoretical cycle time and developed a detailed process flow, it was amazing how many redundant, outmoded, irrelevant steps could be eliminated within and between them. Theoretical cycle time is a dandy yardstick by which to estimate entitlement cycle time in a practical way. Experience over the years reveals that, generally speaking, entitlement is between two and three times theoretical cycle time in manufacturing sectors. In white-collar and service sectors, where baseline cycle times can be very long and theoretical cycle times very short, the ratio is 5 to 10 times theoretical."

Cracking Mindset

At this point, needing to illustrate the basics of Total Cycle Time in as down-to-earth a way as possible, I reached into my grab bag of true anecdotes.

"I started using theoretical cycle time as a measuring tool at Texas Instruments in the sixties, where I was responsible for a line of digital and custom linear circuits. I completely disregarded industry averages and the insistence of my subordinates that we were as competitive as possible. Having determined entitlement on my own, I sought out and eliminated production barriers and hang-ups that were making things take longer than they should. They were everywhere, just as they are in any baseline business, and I had to push hard to break a few logjams.

"Once, for example, my TI line managers gave their assurance that there were no more barriers to remove. However, a look at the production line revealed that there was a machine on that line that constituted a bottleneck because of the time it took to process the large lot sizes it was designed to handle. 'Why are you processing such large lots?' I asked my subordinates. They said they had always done it that way because the machine was served by a carrier that held large lots. 'Get me a saw,' I said. 'I'll cut the damned carrier in half!' We did just that. Lot sizes dropped accordingly, and down came the cycle time again.

"Eventually, I measured a 20 percent gain in labor productivity and a 10 to 15 percent gain in the productivity of equipment. This was important, because the direct-labor costs in that business were 8 percent of sales, and depreciation was about 7 percent of sales. That meant an overall potential gain of 3 percent of sales: $3 million a year in a $100 million business. This was impressive, but at the time it was still not clear to me that the full impact of short cycle time on profitability could be much higher: 15 to 20 percent when cycle time is reduced to entitlement.

"Meanwhile, surprisingly, it turned out that cutting cycle times improved quality. At that time, another curse of the

semiconductor business was low yields. I was delighted to
note, however, that as cycle times plummeted, yields went up.
This, of course, defied conventional wisdom that time-
consuming care enhances quality. The truth was that cutting
the amount of time a product sat on the line reduced the
number of things that could go wrong with it. Yields and
quality climbed.

"Everyone's morale shot up. Our marketing manager
quickly saw the potential of short cycle times and used it to
generate more sales. Designers got excited about the improved manufacturing capability, which allowed them to get
the bugs out of a prototype by running it through the short-
cycle line. The results were astounding: shorter cycle time
and higher motivation enabled the design cycle to drop from
six months to eight weeks. From design through manufacturing, we became at least twice as fast as anyone else in the business. We rolled over the competition. And the entire change
had taken less than a year."

Cycles of Learning and Breakthroughs

"Those kinds of results made me something of a local hero in
the company. Meanwhile, another payoff of short cycle time
operations surfaced: They improved upon themselves. Increasing the number of production cycles in a given period
correspondingly increased the number of learning opportunities which, in turn, offered new clues about how to raise
yields, raise quality, reduce costs, and lower cycle times even
further. By installing a feedback loop to exploit the opportunities short cycle time afforded, we established Cycles of
Learning, which we computed by dividing the number of
work days in a year by the cycle time expressed in days.
Using the example above: when I took over the linear-
custom digital line, it was running at a two-week cycle time
and had undergone about 125 Cycles of Learning since the

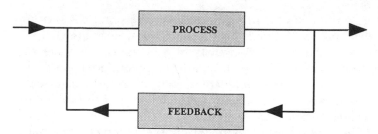

Cycles of Learning: To convert opportunities to learn into increased Cycles of Learning both a creative element and a management forcing function are needed in order to reap the potential benefits of lower costs and higher quality through faster learning.

products' debut. We pushed the cycle time down to eight hours. By that time, the line was experiencing as many Cycles of Learning in two months as the product and process had undergone since its introduction five years before. At the original cycle time, there had been scant opportunity to use Cycles of Learning creatively because people could not honestly remember the details of activities which to them were ancient history. When the cycle time hit entitlement, however, the last cycle's details were still fresh. We learned that to perform satisfactorily, every loop in a Cycle of Learning must include a creative function, an analytical function, and a management driving function. So long as the feedback loop was maintained, the potential for improvement seemed endless."

Three Loops and Five I's

By now I was on a roll, thoroughly enjoying this rehash of those old triumphs.

"For the rest of my career in industry," I continued, "I applied short cycle times and Cycles of Learning to great effect. Gradually, as I moved up the corporate ladder, I realized that those principles applied to all aspects of a business, not merely the manufacturing floor. Over the years, my own organization has defined three major cycles, or loops, that encompass virtually every activity of a business. They are the make/market loop, the design/development loop, and the strategic thrust loop. The three interlock, and within each loop are various cycles, each of which is responsive to the approaches outlined above.

"The make/market loop covers the complete operating business cycle from the time a customer requests a quotation until receivables are collected. Within the make/market loop are such cycles as customer service and cash flow, which encompass numerous subcycles: order entry, forecasting, manufacturing, purchasing, warehousing, and shipping and receivables. Make/market also includes those day-to-day cycles that enable a company to meet total customer requirements, such as merchandising and cost reduction. Most of the make/market loop orbits around customer service. Effective control of that element is fundamental to timely, precise delivery and flexible response to changing customer requirements. Streamline your make/market cycles and you improve your response to your customers' needs. That's why short cycle time culture is the most important weapon in the arsenal of international competition. From our preliminary study, it seems General Widget has a real problem responding to customer needs."

I paused, anticipating questions or maybe even a challenge. There were none. I plunged ahead to the second loop.

"The design/development loop covers the entire process of developing new products, from starting to identify the needs of the marketplace through the realization of cost-effective production. Inside this loop are such cycles as product definition, business commitment, development, and manufacturing. For many businesses, design/development is the crucial loop, for it determines the time to market of a needed product. Shortening the design/development loop's cycle time can have the largest single impact on profitability where development cycles are traditionally long: automobiles and main frame computers, for example."

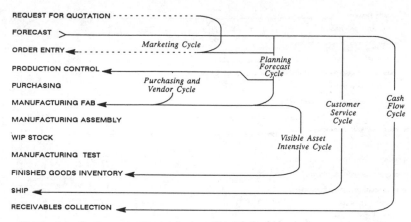

Critical cycle times in the make/market loop.

Thinking of General Widget, I added, "It can also have a whopping impact upon companies where R&D cycle times are longer than the window of opportunity they seek to exploit." I deliberately played with my slides after this statement, stalling while the message sank in. It was very quiet in the General Widget conference room, but I could tell everyone was wide awake. I went on.

"The strategic thrust loop covers activities from the identification of a new business opportunity or area of research to the point where design/development and make/market cycles can take over. Its important cycles include strategic and business development, each containing numerous subcycles.

"Ordinarily, the activity in a company flows from strategic thrust to design/development and then to make/market. The relative importance of make/market, design/development, and strategic thrust obviously varies from business to business. For startup companies, strategic thrust is the most important. In most businesses, including General Widget, the biggest bang for the buck in the short run involves make/market. Two or three years into the future, however, streamlining design/development becomes critical.

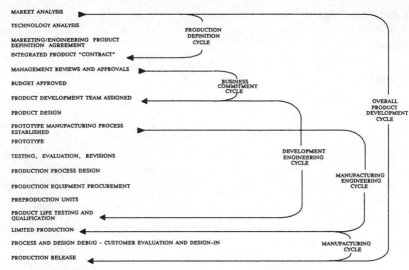

Critical cycle times in the design/development loop.

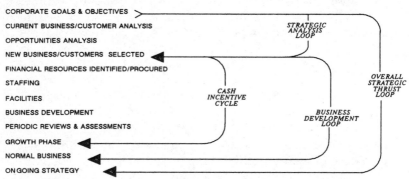

Critical cycle times in the strategic thrust loop.

"Now, these three loops are not independent of one another. They overlap, sharing common areas and subcycles. That's one reason why a broad Total Cycle Time approach is preferable to a piecemeal one. If you people are diffident at this point, I'd recommend you opt for Total Cycle Time in your make/market and design/development loops.

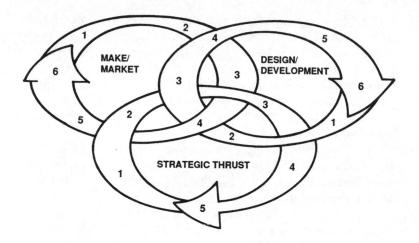

MAKE/MARKET	DESIGN/DEVELOPMENT
FROM CUSTOMER NEED IDENTIFICATION TO PRODUCT/SERVICE DELIVERY	FROM NEW PRODUCT CONCEPT TO COST EFFECTIVE PRODUCTION
1 ORDER ENTRY	1 CONCEPT
2 PLANNING	2 REQUIREMENTS
3 QUALITY	3 DEVELOPMENT
4 ENGINEERING	4 SUPPORT
5 MANUFACTURING	5 PREPRODUCTION
6 ADMINISTRATION	6 ADMINISTRATION

STRATEGIC THRUST

FROM NEW BUSINESS IDENTIFICATION
TO BUSINESS AS USUAL

1 RESEARCH
2 ANALYSIS
3 PLANNING
4 NEW BUSINESS
  START-UP
5 TOTAL CYCLE TIME
  INSTITUTIONALIZATION

Elements in the make/market, design/development, and strategic thrust loops.

"Before we go any farther, I want to stress that moving to Total Cycle Time is much, much more than adopting a 'program.' It's nothing less than changing your corporate culture. Getting to entitlement will require major changes in your methods and attitudes. *Staying* at entitlement requires the acceptance of new measurements and controls that will prevent a relapse. All of this is hard work that doesn't stop when you reach entitlement.

"The process has five overlapping phases called the Five I's: Inspiration, Identification, Information, Implementation, and Institutionalization. Each is a prerequisite for the successful implantation of short cycle time culture. Right now, we are at the *Inspiration* phase, trying to win high-level acceptance at General Widget and revving you up to carry the message to your subordinates.

"*Identification* begins as soon as General Widget says 'yes' to this presentation, at which time we'll pinpoint your make/market and design/development loops cycles and some of the barriers to performance that lie within each. Many of these barriers—customary procedures, redundant steps, people working at cross purposes—are easier for outsiders to spot than insiders.

"Shedding those barriers for keeps requires training. That is the third phase of the Five I's, which for purposes of alliteration is called *Information*."

"As these phases unfold, *Implementation* begins; the term is self-explanatory and involves the identification and removal of barriers.

"During Implementation, the last of the Five I's, *Institutionalization*, comes into play. Institutionalization is nothing less than adopting and living permanently with the mechanisms that preserve Total Cycle Time culture; in particular, the right measurements and controls, plus using the increased Cycles of Learning to realize continuous improvements.

"TGI has developed a "culture change roadmap" to illustrate the relationship between Inspiration, Identification, In-

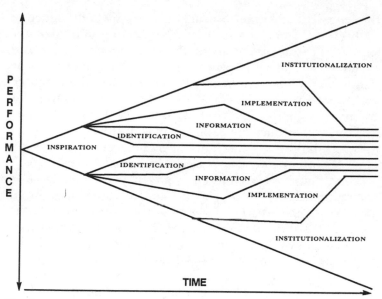

The Five I's Process.

formation, Implementation, and Institutionalization. The Five I's roadmap serves as a constant reminder that the phases of moving to entitlement don't occur in a neat sequence. Once the early inspirational glow starts to dim, the identification of entitlement, the transfer of skills necessary to accomplish the challenge, and the solving of problems become *concurrent* issues. All in all, it is a long haul."

Any Objections?

One or two members of the audience were already finding it a long haul. Prince, who had doggedly penciled geometric doodles all over his copy of my beloved Five I's roadmap, broke into my monologue.

"All this is well and good," he ventured, "but I can't help

thinking of all the other consultants we've sat and listened to in this room who had some sort of airtight program that was supposed to put us ahead of the competition." Nods and smiles from almost everyone followed that comment. "Be that as it may," he continued, "I also can't help thinking that you just don't know General Widget very well. Nobody in this company is complacent, and, as Butch McMills mentioned earlier, our productivity is on a par with the rest of the industry. Who's to say we're not at or near entitlement right now? No offense, but our production figures can't lie."

"No offense," I countered, "but they *can* lie, because you're probably using the wrong measurement indices. In any case, somebody who's operating *above* the industry average is clobbering you in the market, along with the other widget companies you say you're on a par with. If that weren't so, I wouldn't be here. What you call par, I call baseline.

"Now, I know it's going to take awhile to convince you all that you're not already operating at entitlement. In fact, you'd probably be crazy to admit too hastily that you're not using your resources effectively." At this there were a few nervous chuckles. King's gaze, however, never wavered from its lock on me. "Be patient," I said. "There are pleasant surprises on the way that will offset the pain of recognizing that your current performance is not as good as you think. Some parts of General Widget may operate at entitlement. But I have yet to encounter a single case where a client was operating on all cylinders in all loops.

"We have found that baseline performance levels average about 75 percent of entitlement in such areas as productivity, cost, asset utilization, and cash. An overall gain of more than 20 percent in those areas is no trivial matter. Nor is another of our findings: companies that move from baseline to entitlement can expect an improvement in sales of about 10 percent, thanks to improved customer service and time to market. Remember that those improvements are achieved with the resources already on hand.

"I realize that numbers like those look too good to be true, but we're not kidding. Over the years, we've refined a variety of techniques for determining entitlement, including historical analysis, high-low diagnostics, theoretical analysis (which is determining a practical multiple of theoretical cycle time for everyday performance), process databases, and, sometimes, analysis of the competition.

"We're also objective. We can approach a company without the inevitable bias with which insiders rationalize their performance. Please bear in mind that nobody is challenging General Widget's dedication or diligence. But in-house attempts to increase productivity are like self-medication or unsupervised diets. They usually fail because insiders are biased toward their own comfortable norm and therefore can't see the depth of their problem or the strong medicine they need to fix it. By way of example, consider this case—a true one—of a company that had concluded on its own that its order-entry-cycle time of more than twenty days could be trimmed to two. The dramatic reduction was to be achieved by giving sales personnel laptop computers and elaborate software with which to speed up order entry while on the road—admittedly an expensive solution, but necessary, it seemed, for the drastic objective. Our own analysis, however, revealed that by eliminating existing barriers, the company could achieve its order-entry entitlement of approximately three days without making a single new expenditure. Under those circumstances, the purchase of computers and fancy software was unjustifiable.

"A company operating at entitlement can often increase its competitiveness further by adding new resources," I continued, "but such commitments should not be made until *after* entitlement is reached. The spread between baseline, entitlement, and enhanced entitlement can be illustrated handily by the business of document delivery. The U.S. Postal Service, using conventional transportation equipment and facilities, has achieved a delivery time of about three days for first class mail. That is the industry's baseline. Private mail carriers such as Federal Express, through more effective use of sim-

ilar resources, have cut delivery time to about a day, which is
close to the industry's entitlement. Of course, a commitment
to new equipment such as fax machinery can enhance that
entitlement by chopping cycle time to a few minutes.

"Another interesting though less well known example ex-
ists in the building supply area, where baseline for supplying
custom-tempered and insulated glass is three to five weeks.
Entitlement for the industry is about two days. Hunter Glass,
an Oklahoma firm where short cycle time permeates the culture from the front office down, can deliver custom orders
within 300 miles of its plants in forty-eight hours. In this
case, it's difficult to see how the addition of new resources
could improve performance. Customers gladly pay a premium to Hunter again and again, because such service is remembered long after price is forgotten. And who can beat
Domino's Pizza, whose total make/market cycle time of thirty
minutes is the key to its marketing strategy? At Hunter and
Domino, short cycle time is *part of the product*."

Inventory: Some of It You
See, Some You Don't

We took a stretch break at that point, during which General
Widget's management team members confined themselves to
a few polite questions about terminology or fiddled with the
diagrams in their information packets...all except Prudence
Cash, who had obviously done her homework.

"As this company's financial officer, I was intrigued by
your printed comments on cash and inventory, particularly
the concept of invisible inventory," she told me, "but my impression is that they're a little eccentric. How about elaborat-
ing on those issues?" I agreed as we all returned to our seats.
Here was a subject guaranteed to interest everyone present.

"One of the most dramatic aspects of short-cycle-time culture is the cash effect generated by reducing visible and invisible inventory," I began. "*Visible inventory* is accounting-

valued inventory: raw material, work in process, and finished goods on hand. But the accountant's definition of inventory is incomplete, and it can limit management's ability to deal with reality. The fact is that much of the value stored in a corporation is not assigned an accounting value. Unaccounted value can be labeled invisible inventory, a term which covers new designs in process, orders in process, cost-reduction programs in process, receivables in process, and other activities not directly related to accounting-valued inventory.

"A business that moves from long to short cycle times can reduce its visible inventory by one-third to one-half because its response to customer demand is so much quicker. There is simply no need to maintain the backlog of material that once was necessary to meet customer requirements or overcome slipups between order receipt and delivery. Like any manufacturer, General Widget has two types of visible inventory: market-driven and manufacturing-driven. Finished goods and intermediate inventories are market-driven, and are kept on hand to compensate for things that can go wrong during the customer service cycle. How much is stockpiled depends on the nature of your market and the responsiveness of your make/market loop.

"Work-in-process inventory is manufacturing-driven, and is retained to compensate for day-to-day production foulups. Ideally speaking, its quantity is the minimum needed to keep the line balanced. Of course, the amount of inventory of both types is determined by cycle time. Reducing cycle time reduces the amount of both market-driven and manufacturing-driven inventory needed, which amounts to a higher return on assets, increased cash availability, and improved customer service.

"Moving to entitlement will allow you to eliminate unnecessary inventory, which will in turn generate a one-time cash benefit of 3 to 5 percent of sales. That figure is the average of my experience. Depending on circumstances, the figure could be as high as 15 percent. Needless to say, every million dollars worth of flushed inventory contributes a million dollars to more productive uses. As enticing as that sounds, there is a further benefit of overhead reduction. The annual cost of carrying inventory is between 20 and 30 percent of its value per year, depending on the cost of money, obsolescence factors, and the dynamics of the business relative to the inventory. Those savings, too, are not peanuts.

"Now let's talk about invisible inventory. *Invisible inventory* is money spent that is not carried on your company's books but which nonetheless required a cash outlay to put in place. The spending was expensed as incurred and thus had a negative impact upon profit and loss statements. Its importance doesn't necessarily require a change in accepted accounting procedures but does demand a change in management attitudes. New-product development is a classic case. If, for example, a company spends 10 percent of annual sales in this area and products take an average of two years to develop, that company will have 20 percent of annual sales tied up in invisible inventory in that one sector. Or, if a company spends 12 percent of annual sales on selling and marketing and has a one-month order-entry cycle time, 1 percent of total sales is tied up there in invisible inventory. Invisible inventory is calculated by multiplying the spending rate by the cycle time required to achieve results. It is quite possible to free up between 10 and 25 percent of annual sales by reducing invisible inventory through shortened cycle times. Thus, a corporation doing $1 billion in annual sales may have $150 million in visible inventory and between $200 and $400 million worth of invisible inventory in place. If that company cut its cycle times in half, the effective cash impact would amount to $100 to $200 million!"

King had a question: "I know that you're on record as opposing the wholesale adoption of Japanese production techniques, but aren't the Japanese making great strides in reducing inventories with 'just in time' controls?"

King had hit on one of my pet peeves, and I couldn't wait to set him straight: "We've all read about inventory control at a few big companies that Japan, Inc., has milked for all the publicity they're worth," I told him. "In those cases, inventory arrives on the line only at the moment it's needed. But very frequently behind that delivery system stretch lines of trucks going and coming from overstocked 'just in case' warehouses and vendors. In any event, most Japanese plants I have visited operate on long cycle times with large inventories. Recently, I visited a Japanese plant where I was shown the latest nuance of manufacturing ingenuity: a multilayer storage rack that fitted under workers' benches, permitting them to stash three times more inventory than their benchtops could normally hold. Those cluttered racks were seen as a breakthrough! By way of contrast, a U.S. client of mine has a standing rule in one of his plants: minimal benchtops and no storage racks of any kind, period. There is also no appreciable inventory in that plant because there's no place to put it. That's my kind of an organization, and it ought to be your kind as well."

True Cost and True Quality

We turned back to the agenda of the meeting. "Let's talk awhile about cost impacts," I said. "Total Cycle Time will, of course, accelerate cost reduction. But, like inventory, total product cost must be determined in an accurate and meaningful way. Viewed in the Total Cycle Time context, *total product cost* is the sales level less pretax profit divided by the number of products or services delivered. That definition encompasses expenses for research and development, sales and marketing, general and administrative expenses, as well as direct, indirect, variable, and fixed costs. It represents the *real* cost per unit shipped. Low cycle times and low costs go together—to a certain point. It is possible to reduce cycle times so far that costs begin to increase. Generally speaking, manufacturing cost is optimized at two to three times theoretical cycle time. In white-collar areas, the area is five to ten times theoretical.

"As for quality improvement, it would be hard to overstate the impact of Total Cycle Time. In every sector, quality improves as cycle times come down. *Quality* is a function of uncomplicating procedures and eliminating unnecessary steps, inspections, handling, storage, and administration. It is also a function of narrowing distributions and improving predictability of result. It raises first-pass yield: the percentage of actions completed that are done right the first time, eliminating the need for rework or remedial action. Getting back to the Japanese: It's true that long cycle times can produce good quality. Japanese companies ensure their famous high quality by applying detailed statistical quality-control procedures to the subelements of manufacturing, which has established in many minds a link between long cycle times and high quality. I have yet to see a single case where high quality and short cycle time do not go together.

"These days, quality is a magic word and everybody's for it. Admittedly, it can flourish regardless of short cycle time—for a while, at least. The ultimate strategy for General Widget (or any company) should be to adopt a culture where short cycle time and conscious quality improvements coexist as a single culture change: total quality plus Total Cycle Time. That is the best of all worlds."

The Clincher?

My inspirational talk is almost over. "Listen carefully," I said. The cumulative financial impact of Total Cycle Time is proportional to the gap between a company's baseline and entitlement. Accordingly, the bottom-line numbers range from gratifying to astounding. Typically, reaching entitlement will liberate cash to the tune of 10 to 25 percent of annual sales as visible inventories are reduced. Productivity improvement and total-product-cost reduction can range from 10 to 25 percent of sales. As you can see on the range of improvement chart provided, these results are driven by productivity gains

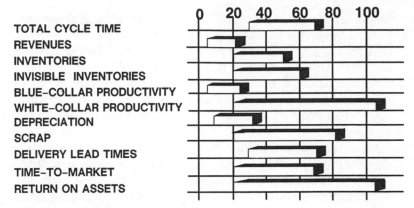

TOTAL CYCLE TIME
REVENUES
INVENTORIES
INVISIBLE INVENTORIES
BLUE-COLLAR PRODUCTIVITY
WHITE-COLLAR PRODUCTIVITY
DEPRECIATION
SCRAP
DELIVERY LEAD TIMES
TIME-TO-MARKET
RETURN ON ASSETS

Ranges of Improvement.

in blue-collar and white-collar areas of 10 to 20 percent and 20 to 100 percent, respectively, along with 15 percent gains in the use of plant and equipment. Total Cycle Time can reduce time to market by 30 to 70 percent. Sales increases from resulting market share gains can vary between 5 and 50 percent.

"All in all, that constitutes a sizable strategic war chest with which to speed new products onto the market, redeploy the work force, and undertake strategic research and development. In the short run, Total Cycle Time catapults a company ahead. In the long run, the culture it embodies will result in a world-class company with ongoing competitiveness and the capability for continuous improvement."

"I feel like saluting the flag," said Hardy Sellers as everyone stood for our well-earned break. That relaxed us enough to dive into the croissants and coffee that had unobtrusively been arranged on a side table.

Prudence Cash, who had had a whispered conversation with King during my inventory remarks, came up to me smiling and said, "If you had just been asked to figure out how much invisible inventory there was in this corporation, where would you start?"

"All in good time," I replied. We were getting through, and I figured we had a friend in Finance.

After we gathered again around the table, I fielded a few questions aimed at relating the generalities of my talk to General Widget, and we made arrangements for me and my team to inspect the facility. Then came a key point in the inspirational program, one that I always insist upon: the CEO's remarks.

"I've spent enough time listening to these guys to know that there's a possibility they can help us," King began. "I'm not altogether sold at this point, but I'm intrigued enough to let them come in and take a look at what we're doing. I'd like you people to cooperate. I've checked their references and confirmed their confidentiality. You may feel free to share anything you have with them. That includes process information, if necessary, and numbers. Make sure you stamp it confidential, but give it to them." The meeting broke up.

A Quick Close-up

We spent the afternoon touring the facility, starting at the spot where orders arrived and moving through the various make/market stations, accompanied by the appropriate managers. Far from being ceremonial, such tours are invariably educational. Because Order Entry was the domain of the marketing VP, Sellers was our first guide.

Looking over the operation, I could not help remarking that the order-entry people were working at a very leisurely pace. "You should see them in a couple of weeks; it'll be nothing but go, go, go!" replied Sellers. Why so? "Well, more orders flow in here at the end of the month than at the beginning." Here was a classic problem that lengthened cycle time.

We were introduced to Sellers's order-entry manager, Marc Squiggle. While we were gathering data about order sizes, orders in process, backlog, and rework, I asked Squiggle for comments. Rework was his pet peeve.

"I don't know what those guys in the field are smokin'," he said, "but half the orders that come in here have only about 80 percent of the details we need. We then have to call them for the other 20 percent. Sometimes they have to call the customer and get back to us. One guy sends orders in here on the last day of the month, just in time for his commission. We never have time to call him back, so we fill in the blanks ourselves to keep things moving and to meet the month's forecast."

Asked about Order Entry's baseline cycle time, Sellers and Squiggle gave twelve days. Some quick calculations told me it was more like sixteen, and I said so. Comparing notes, I discovered that the supervisor's computations had not taken his hold files into account.

"Why should I?" he asked. "Those orders are on hold because of pricing or engineering questions, matters beyond my control. It wouldn't be fair to include them in my department's cycle time." Fair or not, if he chose to exclude them, their long cycle times would never come down. And, fair or not, failure to process those orders on time would count against him with his customers. It really was up to Order Entry to expedite such orders.

For his part, Sellers began to get an eye-opening close-up of cycle time problems in his own division. But the truth was he had already accepted Total Cycle Time in principle. Furthermore, he had taken to heart King's direction to be forthcoming. Like any manager, he was protective of his bailiwick, but being fundamentally a salesperson, he could not repress his conviction that General Widget was missing out on a potential market amounting to several billions of dollars.

"There is nothing fundamentally wrong with our sales force," Sellers said. "It's Manufacturing and Design that are holding us back. Marketing can't get the new products it needs. King and his other VPs don't seem to appreciate the degree to which we're all living on borrowed time, milking our past reputation and my salespeople's good relationships with customers. Those relationships are skidding, however, because it takes forever to get new products out, and when they appear, their quality is a lot lower than the competition's. If you guys are right about short cycle times and high quality, then you have my support. We can sell good stuff, and the quicker the better. Now go try to sell that to Manufacturing. I haven't been able to."

We went to Manufacturing, guided by Prince, VP of Operations and McMills, Manufacturing Manager. Although General Widget's work force appeared well trained, subtle and not-so-subtle whiffs of long cycle times were detectable throughout the operation. Obvious examples were the large lot sizes, long setup times, high rework levels, and the high percentage of down equipment.

We perceived that Prince was amenable to any ideas that would improve performance. But the burden of execution would fall on Butch McMills, who insisted that General Widget's performance problems could not be laid at Manufacturing's door. Despite our elaborate assurances to the contrary, McMills also equated shorter cycle times with speedups. Any other interpretation was contrary to his experience and logic. Manufacturing, he said, already had as much as it could handle. Particularly wedded to the accepted way of doing things, he viewed any big new idea, such as lowered inventory, as a general threat to his proven success.

Getting down to cases, McMills rejected our comment that his work-in-process inventory looked high, saying that such inventory was normal for the business and, more important, essential to his smoothly running line, stable work force, and clean surroundings. He became more defensive when we observed that he had underestimated the real size of his inventory. McMills had conveniently overlooked inventory on hold because of quality, engineering, production planning, or temporary changes in customer needs. His argument reminded us of the Order Entry supervisors': "None of this stuff is my responsibility. It's not Manufacturing's problem, so I discount it." But these problems did indeed affect Manufacturing's cycle time and, in turn, General Widget's response. We counted them in our calculations.

McMills introduced us to Manny Bolster and Moe Fixx, his managers of sustaining engineering and equipment maintenance, respectively. His point in doing so was to demonstrate that both these operations required few resources, which implied that General Widget's manufacturing was under tight control. But most of Bolster's time was spent responding to crises, not in reducing costs. Pointing that out did not ingratiate us with the Manufacturing manager. If General Widget adopted Total Cycle Time, McMills was going to be a tough nut to crack. I made a mental note to summon some outside help.

We fared a bit better at Production Control. Eve Proctor said she'd welcome any new system that simplified the painful interaction between Order Entry and Manufacturing and reduced the flow of customer complaints that piled up on her desk. But we wondered how long a die-hard old-timer like Proctor, who had made a career amongst red tape and time-consuming procedures, would stay on our side if we began to remove too much of the old system.

In Purchasing, L. J. Byer was polite but noncommittal. One item of his data really stood out, however: the inordinately large amounts of inventory purchased from a single supplier, Amalgamated Doodad. The explanation for piling up inventory was simple. That vendor's A-Dad nodules were a key element in almost every General Widget product, yet Amalgamated repeatedly missed delivery schedules. The only safe course, Byer said, was to stockpile A-Dads to cover Amalgamated's unpredictability.

Quality Director Meritt was, like McMills, defensive. His data confirmed his statement that quality at General Widget had indeed climbed. What Meritt could not determine was how General Widget's yields compared to his competitors', notably the Japanese. He seemed satisfied with his historical (baseline) frame of reference and the incremental improvements he had made in the last two years. "Things could be—and used to be—a lot worse," he said.

We also needed to get a handle on research and developmental cycle times in order to put the whole company's performance in perspective. It wasn't easy to corner Dr. Tinker, who had vanished the instant the orientation meeting ended. He gave our team the slip until I spotted him feeding coins to a coffee machine near his office.

"Are you avoiding us?" I asked.

"Look," he replied, "I got your drift during your orientation, but Total Cycle Time doesn't apply to R&D. My people are creative people. The creative process cannot be hurried, and it certainly cannot be roadmapped like an assembly line."

There wasn't enough time to raise Tinker's consciousness over a cup of coffee, which was all the time he could spare. R&D was working flat out, he said, on a new alloy-covered device, the Widgeroo, that had great consumer potential. Accordingly, he excused himself, and we had to settle for his agreement to supply us with raw data.

Regardless of their reactions, all parties gave our team the data we needed. Figures on the Taiwan plant were telecopied to Philadelphia at Prince's request and turned over to us. When we returned to home office, our on-site observations would help us understand why the numbers read the way they did.

What Have We Got Here?

Back in the office ten days later, the TGI team members compared visual impressions and analyzed the General Widget data. We agreed that while employee turnover was low and the company's union relations were not significantly negative, we saw little of the esprit de corps King had described. Our impression was perhaps a function of our outside perspective. Many companies that enjoy consensus culture fail to see the extent to which it can erode over the years. Spontaneous motivation is replaced by institutional slogans and truisms which obscure the changing cultural character.

We did not tarry long in our discussion of key players at General Widget. Clearly, the group contained no empty suits. Although immediate reactions had ranged from enthusiasm (Sellers) to outright hostility (McMills), experience had taught us that people were not the problem, culture was. If we institutionalized Total Cycle Time, it was a safe bet that along the way we would earn unanimous support from General Widget's top managers.

What really absorbed us was the data, which took several weeks to interpret properly. Baselines were established. Theoretical cycle times were determined. High-low analysis of historical cycle times was completed. We analyzed the performance using various approaches to cycle time in each make/market cycle—"entitlement tools"—and brought them to bear on the company's database, using our previous data on similar problems elsewhere to suggest what performance levels were actually attainable. From this, we established entitlement for each of the cycles within the General Widget make/market loop. Meanwhile, we had determined that we needed more in-depth material on R&D because of the strategic importance of new products and the intimate relationships between design/development and make/market. I dispatched a team member back to Philadelphia for that purpose. Ultimately, we were able to produce an accurate assessment of that sector. Of course, the gap between baseline and entitlement varied in magnitude from cycle to cycle within both the make/market and design/development loops, but each of these elements was itemized in the report to General Widget.

Take an example already discussed: Order Entry, which we found to be particularly sluggish. Order Entry's 15-day baseline was established by looking at its current work-in-process inventory and throughput rate. We also analyzed the dates on a large number of orders from the time each salesperson had received the order until that order actually entered into the approved backlog in a form meaningful to planning, purchasing, and manufacturing. Entitlement was established by doing high-low analysis of the order-entry process: looking at the fastest and the slowest orders to go through, and accounting for the differences between those sequences. We also completed a sanity check with a suitable multiplier of the theoretical cycle time we had developed for the process. We then applied the prior experience of the problem-solving team to confirm that our entitlement estimate was realistic. This method was repeated for every cycle. Our results are detailed in the chart shown on pages 54 to 56.

To summarize our findings: moving to entitlement would be a two-year process. General Widget's baseline make/market cycle time was 125 workdays. Its entitlement was 48. Baseline for design/development was 30 months. Entitlement was 16. There was also the potential for a companywide 24 percent gain in productivity.

At baseline, the company's revenue per person was $92.3 thousand, a respectable but unspectacular figure. At entitlement, it would rise to $114.5 thousand, a gain in revenue per person of 24 percent. Baseline return on assets, 4.5 percent, would rise to 15.9 percent at entitlement, a gain of 250 percent.

Some other figures: the value of visible inventory would decrease from $95 million to $78 million. (We estimated that without Total Cycle Time, the baseline figure would rise to almost $118 million in two years.) Invisible inventory would fall from $270 million to $202 in the same period (or, without culture change, it would rise to $331 million.)

General Widget's pretax profits would increase from $30 million to $112 million, a 273 percent improvement. Its profits after taxes would rise from $18 million to $67 million. Here were the kinds of numbers that, without our supporting detail, looked too good to be true, especially as they required no investment of new resources. Now came the climactic point for both the Inspiration and Identification phases at General Widget: formal presentation of our assessment.

Coffee and Culture Change

King had received a brief advance rundown of our report, which he shared with his financial VP, but he had decided to have us present the material to the rest of his top and middle managers, seventy in all, in order to maximize initial understanding of the many charts we had devised. He took the further precaution of telephoning me to say that I might expect a bit of opposition.

"Since your first presentation," he explained, "we've been doing a little analysis of our own, and some of us are convinced that we're operating close to entitlement right now. Sure, there's room for improvement—I wouldn't have contacted you if I didn't believe that—but after our self-examination, we're not sure how much good you can do us. The figures in your study are going to astound one or two of our key people."

A six-hour meeting was scheduled to be held in the Betsy Ross Room of a motor hotel on a commercial strip near the General Widget complex. In addition to the people who had attended our first meeting, the CEO had crowded his entire corporate staff into the General Widget conference room to hear TGI's presentation of its findings.

A presentation of this sort involves the same sort of psychological problems I had encountered in my first talk at General Widget. One, of course, is the initial exposure to an objective calibration of baseline and entitlement figures, which often inspire disbelief. The other is the possible inference by believers that the figures reflect badly on their competence. There is no way around these problems, so I usually go straight ahead.

"To begin with," I said after King had introduced me, "I assume you are dead serious about raising the company's competitiveness in the markets you serve. Please consider what follows as outside constructive criticism. TGI is objective and does not sugarcoat its pills. You may not be altogether pleased by what you hear this morning, but try to

GENERAL WIDGET COMPANY
BASELINE VERSUS ENTITLEMENT
(IN CONSTANT DOLLARS)

PROFIT AND LOSS STATEMENT

	Baseline (Const. $)	Entitlement (in 2 years)	Change Dollars	Change Percentage
Sales	$600M	$750M • Market share Customer service 10% • Market share Time to market 15% • Equipment utilization (15% utilization, 10% additional capacity)	$150M	25%
Design/ development	12% of sales	12% of sales (50% productivity gain— effectively 18%)	—	—
Marketing	10% of sales	8% (effectively 12.5% of sales with productivity gain of 25%)	$15M	25%
Pretax profit	$30M	$112M	$82M	273%

Tax rate	40%	40%		—
Profit after taxes	$18M	$67M	$49M	172%
Return on assets	4.5%	15.9%		253%

PEOPLE-RELATED INDICES

Revenue/person	$92.3K	$114.5K (+24% productivity gain)	$22.2K	24%
Employees	6,500	6,550		(7%)
Manufacturing people	3,700	3,850 (20% productivity gain)		
Indirect people	2,800	2,700 (30% productivity gain)		
Annual turnover	10% direct labor 5% indirect labor			

KEY BALANCE SHEET ITEMS

Total assets		
Cash	10M	10M
Visible inventory	95M	78M
Receivables	82M	103M
Plant, property, and equipment	213M	230M

GENERAL WIDGET COMPANY
BASELINE VERSUS ENTITLEMENT
(IN CONSTANT DOLLARS)

KEY BALANCE SHEET ITEMS (*CONTINUED*)

	Baseline (Const. $)	Entitlement (in 2 years)	Change Dollars	Change Percentage
Equipment	133M	150M	($21M)	(5.3%)
Plant	80M	80M		
	$400M	$421M	(avoid $79M)	
Visible inventory	$95M	$78M ($118.7M if not improved)	$17M (avoid $40.7M)	18% (43%)
Invisible inventory	$270M	$202M ($337M if not improved)	$68M (avoid $135M)	26% (40%)
	45% of sales	27% of sales		

CYCLE-TIME-RELATED INDICES

	Baseline (Const. $)	Entitlement (in 2 years)	Change Dollars	Change Percentage
Make/market cycle time (Order Entry)	110 workdays (15 days)	45 workdays (3 days)		60% 80%
Design/development cycle time	30 months	16 months (+80% productivity gain)		47%
Customer service	80%	95%		18%

56

accept the inputs, because you are on the threshold of an enormous opportunity."

As I went through the baseline and entitlement figures, the loudest noise in the room was the sound of the projector fan. Next came our proposal, presented in the form of a two-year roadmap.

At 10 a.m., King announced that coffee was being served downstairs but that everyone was to reconvene promptly in 15 minutes. As luck would have it, the break afforded me an opportunity to demonstrate a few of the points at issue. All 70 attendees went downstairs and into a small room, where a single waiter stood behind a table set with two urns, requisite cups and saucers, sugar, cream, and generous plates of sweet rolls. Noticing this situation, I timed the waiter. He took 8 seconds to pour each cup of coffee and 18 to produce a cup of tea. Adding cream or sugar held up the line another three seconds. Assuming a 10-to-1 ratio of coffee to tea, I did a little multiplication and decided there was no way everyone could sip, munch, smoke, stop at the rest rooms, and make it back upstairs by 10:15. While the attendees were thus engaged, I escaped to the Betsy Ross Room and made a slide for the overhead projector that read "I PREDICT THAT THE COFFEE BREAK CYCLE TIME IS 21 MINUTES AND THAT WE WILL RESTART AT 10:21." I put it on the projector, turned the machine on, and went downstairs for a cup of tea.

People began filing in at about 10:18, looking at the slide, then at their watches, then at the entrance. Sure enough, at 10:20, the last straggler hurried in, finishing off a bite of chocolate doughnut. It took her a minute to see why everyone was laughing. When things quieted down, King asked aloud why and how I had made so accurate a prediction.

"I wanted to show you that the most mundane activities can be analyzed well enough to predict their outcome and adjust accordingly," I explained. I quickly drew and projected a flowchart diagram to illustrate the breakdown of the coffee situation. "We've got a cycle time problem right here.

How do we fix it?" In no time, the group had decided we needed three waiters for the afternoon break, and one of their number headed for the front desk to make the proper request.

When we got back to business, King spoke first. "General Widget prides itself on being an open forum for management. As you all know, we don't make big moves without consensus, although sometimes that has cost us dearly. Total Cycle Time is a big and permanent move. I support it. But it won't fly unless key people commit themselves to its principles. Now is the time to go on record."

King's measured, serious tone left little doubt about where he stood or that the time for casual observations had passed. Unless there was serious division within the top ranks, General Widget would go for Total Cycle Time.

Hardy Sellers stood up, said "Let's do it!" and sat down. That was undoubtedly the shortest speech in the garrulous marketeer's career. It generated a few laughs and lightened the mood.

Prudence Cash: "I've had a chance to run through the advance draft of this report. One of the most important things it tells me is that Total Cycle Time is virtually self-supporting, so it will not work a financial hardship on the company. But there is more. As you all know, we've been biting our nails about where to find funding to grow the company through its next $150 million. Well, by flushing visible and invisible inventory—and I now know where to find both types—we'll accumulate enough cash to virtually support our growth objectives internally. One other financial point: all of us here participate in a stock option plan, so I don't have to paint you pictures to illustrate what a 250 percent gain in General Widget's return on assets will do for stock values."

Murmurings, then there was an awkward silence. The CEO looked at Prince, who looked at McMills. McMills stood up. "When it comes to the entitlement for Manufacturing, I've got to admit, I'm from Missouri. My instincts still tell me that we can't get to entitlement on current resources, or we'd be nearer that figure now. But I've checked around, and TGI has satisfied me that General Widget's entitlement figures are not out of line with entitlements elsewhere. If we have reasonable consensus, I'll go with it."

McMills had put his hostility on hold, but Hunter Meritt had not. The quality manager's only comment was, "Quality takes care, and care takes time. The faster we run, the more likely we are to make errors." My response was that he had underestimated the exponential effect of Cycles of Learning on first-pass yield and overall quality. He did not argue, but I could see he was unconvinced.

The only other comment came from Dr. Tinker. TGI's recent return to General Widget for more data had made Tinker realize that we were dead serious about shortening research and development cycles, and he was, he said, alarmed. "Look. I've been working with creative people for years. I'm a creative person myself, and I tell you that short cycle times will not fly in R&D. The last thing I can tell my people is that I'm going to double their productivity. They'll quit and go somewhere else. They don't want to be measured by a stopwatch. They shouldn't be measured by a stopwatch. How do I handle this? You say that they'll work at the same rate over half the hurdles. What hurdles?"

Because all eyes were on me, I ventured to answer Tinker's question in a general context. "First of all, you don't announce that you're going to double productivity in R&D. Say instead that you are going to find ways to make the development process easier. That has got to appeal to your people, because much of their process is hurry-up-and-wait.

"If you adopt Total Cycle Time, it will be our responsibility to analyze the flow of products through General Widget, looking at the hurry-up pieces and the wait pieces. Then we get rid of the points where no value is added. Research and Development is no different in that regard from any other corporate element. You do experiments and you await results. You design an experiment and wait for a chance to run it. You design a prototype and wait for the model shop to produce an example. And you wait and wait. We've noted that General Widget's model shop is a real barrier to smooth operations. The people there have established an unhurried pace and they like it that way. How many signatures does it take to authorize a model in that shop? Ten? Why not two? How many of those sign-offs are there for irrelevant historical reasons or for ego gratification? Consider: the model shop's cycle time can be reduced by 80 percent, and I'll bet there isn't a single creative person in R&D who wouldn't cheer if that happened.

"We are proposing to oversee a major, permanent culture change at General Widget. That includes educating and transferring a set of skills to the people in that model shop and to every other business cycle in the company. As you will see from the roadmap diagram in your packets, we call that phase Information, and it interlocks with Implementation and Institutionalization. We're talking about two years of major effort that involves everyone, starting with Mr. King over here and extending all the way down to operators on the manufacturing floor and maintenance personnel, and out to Taiwan."

Silence. A few people rooted in their information packet for the roadmap. Others looked at its projected image on the screen. King spoke. "I feel positive, but I want to talk this over with my people. At the moment, I'm concerned about the objections I've heard, which I'm sure will multiply as we go down the ladder. This company operates by consensus, not force."

"I would be absolutely amazed if you got unanimity at the outset," I answered. "And there will also be opposition along the way. Moving from baseline to entitlement is analogous to lowering the water in a lake. As the level falls, it exposes rocks that must be removed for smooth sailing. As it falls farther, another set of rocks is likely to appear. At General Widget, some of those rocks represent the incompetence of people. Others represent people's innate reluctance to abandon the familiar. People like the comfort of the status quo, they like the comfort of history, or they like the comfort of inventory. Change equals discomfort. Frankly, I think we have seen some of that here today. In any case, you are bound to encounter consensus problems as you proceed. Most of these are temporary."

Meeting King's gaze, I said, "We're talking about nothing less than a fundamental change in your corporate culture. You must decide if this is what you want to do. If you decide it is, then there will be times when you will have to insist that people march to the new cadence. That's what culture change is all about, and you can't get Total Cycle Time without that kind of direction. When you've institutionalized such a culture you can expect to end up with a market-responsive, high-quality, low-cost culture. That will breed its own consensus."

Looking back, I realize it might not have been politic to put King's consensus preoccupations on the line in front of his assembled subordinates. It was also risky from the standpoint of the proposal's acceptance. But there was no way around the cultural issue. So long as General Widget people up and down the line could withhold support for whatever reason, Total Cycle Time would not take.

King said it was time for a decision. He brought the meeting to a close, then excused us for two hours while he and his staff conferred. When he and I reconvened in his office, he said, "We just went over the pros and cons again," he said. "It became obvious to us all that it is easier to sit and pay lip service to principles than to implement them. We could talk forever. I've decided to get started right away. I would prefer to proceed on a primarily incentive arrangement. Is an incentive plus travel expenses arrangement okay with you?"

It was okay. By the incentive arrangement, most of our fee would be tied to General Widget's measurable progress, thereby eliminating the company's risk and placing both parties in a win-win partnership.

I told King General Widget would have the details within two weeks. "Short cycle times must become a way of life, even at the expense of consensus. We'll put together a problem-solving team and prepare to get under way in five weeks. I will lead the team. We'll probably split our time roughly evenly between working here in Philadelphia, where we identify barriers and implement solutions, and at our own headquarters, where we analyze and develop those solutions."

On the following day, I briefed the company's senior management on getting started. "Who do you suggest I assign to the program as General Widget's program manager?" King asked.

"Nobody!" I replied. "Total Cycle Time is not a program. If you, as CEO, set up a program office and designate someone as the Champion of Total Cycle Time, it isn't going to work. It is these people: the VPs of Finance, Operations, Marketing, R&D, and so on, who with their staffs are going to change General Widget. Practically speaking, our people will most often have to interface with your make/market and design/development leadership."

"Then Prince and Tinker are your focal points."

"Hold it a second," exclaimed Prince, who may suddenly have seen some writing on the wall. "It looks like we'll be paying you for part-time work around here. I'll want your people here, where I can see them and interact with them at all times."

"If my organization takes over, moves to the center ring, and brings General Widget to entitlement, what do you do when we leave?" I asked Prince. "Your organization has to accomplish Implementation. Otherwise, Total Cycle Time culture will not be properly institutionalized. We describe ourselves as coaches and catalysts. We break logjams and guide your people as they come up with solutions. We train your people, no matter how long it takes. We guide them. But we do not do the kind of work they are in the organization to accomplish. And when it's time for us to ride off into the sunset, your people will know what was done to reach entitlement. Just as important, they will feel that they did it. If all this is done right, the new culture will be owned by your people and will stay in place, and General Widget will wonder what the heck TGI did here."

"Already I'm beginning to feel the brunt of your comment that Total Cycle Time is easy to believe in but difficult to accomplish," said King. "And I'll learn to watch my terminology carefully in the future, at least in front of you and your team! But time is short." King rose and everyone else made to do likewise. "Sellers, would you repeat your little speech as I make my getaway?"

Sellers stood up exactly as he had before. "Let's DO it!" he said. Only this time, instead of sitting down, he laughed and headed for the door in King's wake. So did everybody else.

Results: A Graphic Display

That evening, I was scheduled to join Victor King for what I knew would be a first-class dinner. Meanwhile, waiting in the hotel lobby, I mulled over the day's events and the progress made. What had lately transpired was typical of many other episodes during the Inspiration and Identification phases. Most prospects quickly appreciate the importance of time as a competitive weapon and accept intellectually the principles of Total Cycle Time. Who, after all, will argue with such motherhood issues as improved customer response, better utilization of resources, and shortened time to market? That first approval, however, often turns into disbelief when customers see our baseline and entitlement figures. Their reactions are understandable. In the first place, they are confident that their accustomed performance level is close to optimal, so they are frankly suspicious of entitlement projections that seem wildly optimistic and, incidentally, suggest that they have not been performing as well as they thought.

To improve credibility during Inspiration meetings, we make sure that every participant's information packet contains explanations of the method used for determining baseline and entitlement. Our projections are carefully calculated from historical analysis, an examination of the company's high-priority cycle times, and multiples of theoretical cycle time.

We also use diagrams to illustrate our rationale. Before General Widget's top managers were polled for their support, all had seen the two that appear below and on the following page. The first shows the distribution of expected results at various cycle times, and speaks to management's need to improve the predictability of results so that a customer can know exactly when to expect a quality product. Notice that at baseline there is poor predictability and a very long "tail" of ever-slower results.

Now consider the diagram showing multiples of theoretical cycle time. As I mentioned above, suitable multiples in the manufacturing area are two to three times the theoretical cycle time and in administrative processes are 5 to 10 times theoretical. As the chart on page 65 shows, getting cycle times to their optimum multiple of theoretical will bring first-pass yield and overall quality to their highest practical levels while dropping costs to their lowest.

Explanations and diagrams usually persuade skeptics that our predictions are credible, but the Inspiration phase packs a few other negative reactions that must also be quickly over-

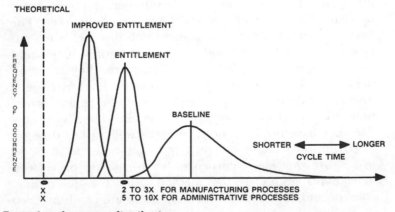

Typical performance distributions.

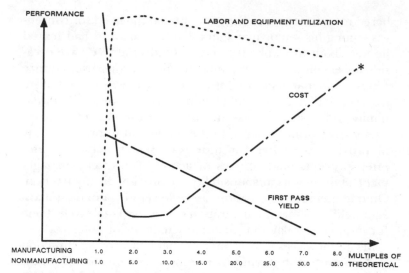

The relationship of cost to first-pass yield, labor and equipment utilization as a function of multiples of theoretical. (Note that cost rises as theoretical is approached.)

come. One is the you-don't-understand-my-business syndrome, in which the listeners admit that Total Cycle Time is a good idea in most cases but that their line of work is an exception.

Another hazard of the Inspiration phase is a function of the enthusiasm it often engenders. Participants, eager for quick results, decide to undertake Total Cycle Time on their own as a crash program. But such programs rarely meet expectations because its protagonists are too close to the issues and problems. Accordingly, their objectivity is compromised. Insiders can probably spot and fix a number of problems in their area of expertise, but they will have little luck identifying and overcoming process barriers. And it is asking too much of an organization steeped in its own culture to spot and expunge the cultural elements that are doing it harm. Obviously, Victor King had ruled out self-medication before his first telephone call to me.

Reviewing the day's events at General Widget, I remembered my anxiety when King mentioned the need for consensus among his senior managers. For a moment, I had feared he was about to invoke the buy-in syndrome. We have occasionally encountered companies steeped in consensus culture where all managers must "buy into" any new concept before it is accepted. The principle behind such thinking is that unanimity will ensure success and preserve the individual manager's sense of importance to the whole, but in practice, buy-in provides a shelter for indecisive senior managers and often prevents bold courses of action. Too often, management abdicates its responsibility to provide firm direction. On one memorable occasion, a single veto by a middle manager held up a major corporation's plan for Total Cycle Time for months, a delay that cost many millions of dollars.

Most employees expect management to provide direction and do not relish having to rule on every nuance of a new program. Our meeting with King and his subordinates had convinced me that General Widget's CEO liked to solicit opinions, but did not require unanimity to make a big decision. I also knew that, if necessary, I could count on King to apply his top-down power to dislodge future obstructions.

All in all, Inspiration at General Widget had proceeded more than satisfactorily. But as has been said repeatedly, Total Cycle Time is easy to understand intellectually and hard to enact. Inevitably, the first flush of enthusiasm wanes as the initial barriers are exposed. People then realize that the road to entitlement is a steep one. With time, the waning inspirational enthusiasm is replaced by satisfaction over results. In between, the going can be rough.

Such an inspirational dilemma is analogous to weight loss. The task of an overweight dieter is conceptually very simple. All he or she has to do is eat less and exercise more and pounds will eventually disappear. At first, the novelty of the program and high expectations provide motivation. Later, the visible results keep the momentum going. The trick for most dieters is not shedding pounds but changing the context of their entire lives to prevent future weight gain. In the

long run, few can make the transition to a lower weight culture. Total Cycle Time is not a miracle two-week diet. It is an
organized, systematic plan in which old, flabby practices,
shed forever, are replaced by a new, lifetime regimen.

The Meat of the Business

My fashionably late dinner with Victor King took place at a
small, elegant restaurant in Philadelphia's quaint but pricey
Society Hill district. We dawdled over coffee. In the wake of
the day's meeting, and on the brink of a major change in his
company's culture, King pressed me for inspirational anecdotes. That was all the pretext I needed to trot out a favorite.

"One of the most interesting cases I've witnessed involved
the president of a large meat packing business," I began.
"The CEO had heard about our work and wanted proof that
Total Cycle Time was applicable everywhere. True to my
convictions, I agreed to visit one of his plants, where I was to
deliver a 45-minute lecture on Total Cycle Time and, after a
quick look around, estimate the operation's baseline and entitlement. I had never set foot in a meat packing plant before,
which must have become obvious to all concerned when I arrived in a spotless white shirt.

"My first stop was at the office of the plant manager and
his two immediate subordinates. On their good behavior, all
three assured me that they were interested in any ideas I
might have about improving their operation. They readily
supplied whatever data I needed, but they were clearly
doubtful that my world had anything to teach theirs. Here
was their world: Live cows and steers walked into one end of
a big building, and steaks, chops, and roasts came out the
other.

"The tour of the facility was fascinating, although it was
not an excursion suitable for everybody, and I wouldn't be
telling you the tale if you hadn't already finished your filet
mignon. The purposeful activity of the place was obvious

even as I drove up. A column of cattle trucks was noisily un-
loading livestock into holding pens, animals were being
sprayed with water to prevent last-minute weight loss, and at
the other end of the building, a second line of vehicles were
loading boxed steaks and chops.

"The plant was organized into three basic units. One of
these, aptly named the "kill" department, received the live
animals, slaughtered them, and delivered sides of beef into a
huge refrigerator that occupied most of the building's space.
As part of the process, the kill department removed from
each animal carcass the head, horns, hoofs, hide, and anything else considered inedible and routed those items off to
appropriate resale locations. The department received so
much per side and whatever revenue these by-products
brought. Believe me, nothing was wasted.

"The sides hung in the cooler for about 18 hours. Then,
on a first-in, first-out basis, they entered the packing department, where they were divided into steaks, ribs, and various
other cuts that were weighed, boxed, and loaded onto refrig-
erated trucks.

"Cycle times? I calculated that from the moment an animal
walked into the building until it was two sides of beef entering the cooler, 27 minutes elapsed. Not bad! The 18-hour
cooler time was precisely the amount of time necessary to
achieve the optimum USDA rating, so that too seemed efficient. Packing's cycle time was even more impressive than the
kill department's: 22 minutes from whole sides of beef to
packaged cuts going out the back door. That was one of the
shortest cycle times I had ever experienced, and my initial
impression was that there was little that could be done to improve profitability. But I was wrong. Upon examining the
measurements and controls data, which were minutely detailed, it became apparent that there was substantial room for
improvement.

"The plant was running as a one-shift operation, with the
cooler bridging the overnight lull. Needless to say, despite
the short cycle times of the kill and packing departments, the

actual one-shift cycle time for the entire operation was close to 19 hours. That meant that everyone had 240 Cycles of Learning per year, yet they had never taken advantage of a single one—nary a feedback loop in the plant, nor a management forcing function to squeeze out a little performance improvement. The figures on scrap were out of line; there was too much. I noted quite a lot of downgrading of meat, caused by a failure in kill to match the needs in packing. Year in and year out, the plant had rushed along, doing things the same way. In my report, I estimated that the plant's profitability could be improved to the tune of $6 million a year if an appropriate creative feedback loop was put in place. Think of it: 240 opportunities a year in which to improve performance!"

"So the moral of your story is that short cycle times alone may not bring a business to entitlement, right?" said King as he picked up the check.

"Yes," I agreed. "And since General Widget is still in its Inspiration phase, I wanted to inspire you with one last lesson: You can get pretty efficient by shortening cycle times, but if you use Cycles of Learning and feedback loops, your performance improvement will climb past your original entitlement goal. Somewhere out there is a lean and mean meat packing plant exploiting that opportunity. Hey, all this talk is making me hungry. Is there an all-night place nearby where we could grab a hamburger?"

3
Results

The size of the team assigned to General Widget varied from four to ten people, depending on which sets of skills were needed from time to time. The team's implementation process was analogous to the peeling of an onion. First, we reverified our baseline and entitlement estimates for every make/market and design/development cycle at General Widget. Then we had to develop detailed understanding of the actual business processes involved, rank-order the barriers obstructing entitlement, train personnel, and oversee removal of obstructions. As those barriers disappeared and cycle times declined, new barriers would surface. Then, the sequence would begin again.

Hitting a major barrier while reducing cycle time within a process creates a new performance plateau which, while an improvement over baseline, is still short of entitlement. Most plateaus are caused by cultural or business process barriers against which falling cycle time levels off. With cycle times left unattended, there is a distinct possibility that they will creep back toward baseline. Maintaining momentum across each new plateau is a major challenge.

General Widget's order-entry process, cited previously, affords a good example of Implementation and its problems.

As has been seen, order-entry manager Marc Squiggle de-
nied at first that his operation had a problem. Order Entry
operated on one shift. Squiggle found our entitlement estimate of three days very aggressive against his own calculation
of fifteen, even though he had walked emergency orders
through the process in two and a half days. A separate, detailed analysis of the order-entry process had established
one-order theoretical cycle time at 2.4 hours. Using our multiple of 5 to 10 for white-collar theoretical to entitlement, we
arrived at a 12- to 24-hour range. We set entitlement at less
than three days.

By telling Squiggle a bevy of unidentified but pertinent
war stories from our company annals, my team was at last
able to persuade him that the current process could stand
some revision. I knew that as headway was made against
those long-standing barriers, new ones would surely surface.
But if Squiggle's team played ball, entitlement would eventually be reached. By tracing rework back through the pipeline
to locate the source of error, we could demonstrate to Squiggle that Order Entry's process contained too many nonvalue
added steps. As was typical, Order Entry employed several
time-consuming checks and balances within its process and
an equivalent number of delays as orders made their way to
and from these stations.

I asked Squiggle what he thought was his biggest problem
aside from rework. He answered after a moment's reflection:
"I'm reluctant to say this outright, but it's right here in Marketing. Generally speaking, Marketing is a gung-ho, aggressive organization, yet we have to wait about six days for a
turnaround on pricing approval." One of our team members
and Squiggle examined that process, and concluded its theoretical cycle time looked to be about 25 minutes! Even at ten
times theoretical, pricing approval should be completed in
five hours, not six days.

By splitting the pricing approval process up into its components, we isolated the tie-ups. For example, Marketing
people insisted on receiving orders in a batch, and would not

sit down and price out orders in batches of less than a hundred. Why? Because they believed that batch processing was the most efficient way to utilize their resources. A second problem followed: Once batches were processed, they were subjected to an approval cycle that required five signatures. A third problem was personal: There had been enough friction between salespeople and order-entry people to cause the former to regard their autonomy as a matter of territorial rights, not subject to criticism from other departments.

This complicated situation had historical roots. Five years before, there had been several painful instances of careless mispricing, and an edict had gone out from Sellers that henceforward all price approvals were to be scrutinized by senior management. That may also have prompted the practice of letting paperwork pile up into batch lots of a hundred. We, however, concluded that the large lot sizes were a matter of comfort levels: price approvers felt more secure with stacks of work on their desks. If the stacks went down, their jobs might appear redundant. In any case, although the crisis had long since passed, Order Entry was being made to wait purposelessly for a mostly ceremonial routing of paperwork.

We persuaded Squiggle to sit down with Goldie Buck, his counterpart in Price Approval, and analyze the way out of such a mess. Their risk-versus-approval analysis turned up a more rational approach to sign-offs. General Widget orders averaged about $5000 each, although occasionally an order might be as high as $1 million. Squiggle decided to push for a revision of the rules to allow any orders under $50,000 to be expedited without executive signatures. Reducing the batch barrier took a little longer. When the results of shortened cycle time increased the load on Manufacturing, a now-redundant Price-Approval clerk was redeployed to that sector, and, simultaneously, the 100-order batch-lot size was officially eliminated by Vice President Sellers. With practice, a cycle time of five hours was indeed achievable in Price Approval.

Remedying internal tie-ups at Order Entry took months. Squiggle and one of my teammates set up a Total Cycle Time equivalent of a "quality circle" consisting of experienced clerks and credit approval specialists. After hearing how important it was for General Widget to streamline its order-entry process—TGI's dollar impact figures were cited—participants were encouraged to talk about what steps obstructed short cycle time. This they could do handily. They pinpointed the error rate, the overabundant check-and-balance stations, and the time-consuming waits as orders made their way to and from stations.

On the strength of those recommendations, we had Squiggle set up a single, experimental cell that would handle every process step. A portion of the incoming orders were diverted to that cell. Immediately, the "white spaces," into which orders had been disappearing as they made the rounds, vanished. The cell was provided with its own small copying machine, which eliminated reliance on General Widget's central copying center and a lot of multiple-form paperwork in the bargain. Errors declined, obviating the need for most accuracy checks. The six-day cycle time dropped by a day and a half.

There it stuck, a long way from the half-day cycle time that had been defined as entitlement. One morning, in search of a free cup of coffee, I came upon Squiggle, scowling as he shook a packet of ersatz cream into his cup. I asked him what was wrong.

"The cell isn't working," he replied. "We made a little progress, but we're stopped and can't figure out how to get things going again."

And how were things in Price Approval? "Well, we took care of that," he answered. "People are now getting used to the new process. Penny Halt and Nichols Bloch come to the cell, pick up orders, and provide the verification we need."

Immediately, alarm bells went off in my head. Penny Halt and Nick Bloch were Price-Approval clerks who had been with General Widget since the year one and whose knowledge of the products was almost intimidating. But they had been kingpins of the old, roundabout Price-Approval routine and had defended the old batch lots and routing procedures that had been abolished. Based on numerous experiences elsewhere, I was willing to bet that Penny and Nick were still operating in the old manner, letting orders accumulate into reassuring piles of work on their desks. My suspicions were confirmed by Goldie Buck when she attended Order Entry's next cycle time reduction meeting. The two Price-Approval clerks had indeed become barriers against which descending cycle time had stopped.

Penny and Nick were also a classic case of how "worker bees" accustomed to a routine often resist and disrupt change that has been decreed from on high. I had seen similar cases dozens of times in other companies. From our point of view, we had failed to implement properly the new culture in their area, and they clung to procedures they had lived with, and believed in, for years. I am sure they were convinced that on their own initiative, they were acting in the best interests of General Widget, notwithstanding the mandated changes.

Here was a touchy issue. Both clerks were senior employees with meritorious records, and the last thing we wanted to do was embarrass them. Furthermore, they possessed a wealth of expertise about General Widget's customers. The trick was to turn that expertise to advantage. I therefore suggested to Squiggle that he and Buck redeploy the two clerks elsewhere, where their experience would be of benefit and their reflexive proceduralism would die a natural death. Squiggle, of course, did not look forward to confronting Buck about matters that were the latter's domain. His choice of action, I thought, was rather savvy: He arranged a private meeting with Buck in Vice President Sellers's office. Squiggle knew that once the situation was made clear to Sellers, action would follow immediately. Squiggle also knew that Sellers was probably the best negotiator and psychologist in the organization, and could ameliorate wounded professional pride.

Squiggle told me later that at the meeting, Sellers raised the flag of the general good for General Widget, painting rosy pictures as though the Price-Approval problem were another golden opportunity for all concerned to show the right stuff. In an ironic decision worthy of Solomon, he persuaded Squiggle and Buck that the best course of action was to transfer Penny Halt and Nichols Bloch to Order Entry. Such a move was not a demotion, and it could be rationalized by the fact that their expertise would raise the skill level of the very organization whose progress they had been obstructing. Specifically, he asked Squiggle to assign them to the experimental cell. It worked. Given more responsibility, the remaining Price-Approval clerks adapted readily to the new procedures. With another barrier removed, Order Entry's cell continued its movement toward entitlement.

The revelations of the experimental cell prompted Sellers and Squiggle to reorganize all of Order Entry into self-contained cells. Doing so would improve quality, reduce costs, and virtually eliminate overtime. Reorganization, however, exposed an external condition that, under the new system, was intolerable: briefcase inventory and briefcase cycle time. As always, orders arrived unevenly, dribbling in during the early part of each month, then piling up at the end, as salespeople dumped their paperwork. The crunch at the end of each month caused delays and errors in processing. Sellers found it difficult to change his sales force's habits, however. At the company's annual sales meeting, sales managers immediately grasped the benefits of short cycle time: better customer service and an end to the order tracking that consumed time they would rather spend on selling. But, as good as it sounded to go-getters in Sales, turning understanding into action was another matter. As Sellers put it, "Paperwork is not the average salesperson's forte. He or she will, out of force of habit, haul valuable orders around in a briefcase until commission time looms up. We've got to provide an incentive." Or, in accordance with TGI-management philosophy, we had to institutionalize a change in culture.

Sellers adopted a new measurement format in which sales-persons would report every sale at the time it was made. If, after a week, the order had not arrived in Philadelphia, offending parties received a telephone call from the home office wanting to know why. Promptness became one of the criteria by which the sales force was evaluated. After the new culture sank in, Sales and Order Entry struck a bargain: If salespersons would reduce their order entries from an average of five days to one, the home office would process them in two additional days.

To ensure institutionalization of the changes, Sellers, Squiggle, Buck, and I drew up a general set of new marketing cycle time performance measurements for Marketing which King, as CEO, accepted as part of the company's regular monthly business review.

War Stories and WIP

Over in Manufacturing, we had anticipated at least lukewarm acceptance of Total Cycle Time. But here, more than in Order Entry, we encountered stiff resistance. In the first place, Butch McMills refused flat out to accept TGI's entitlement figure for the manufacturing line: 16 days instead of baseline's 33. At the meeting where we gave out the news, you could at first have heard a pin drop but for the clatter and hiss of the machinery on the other side of the conference room wall. Then, suddenly, all of McMills's supervisors wanted to speak at once. In the words of one, "Our present cycle time is better than it has ever been since General Widget was founded. Okay, maybe we could knock off a day or two more. But 16 days?! It's hard to take a number like that seriously."

Then McMills himself hit us where it hurt, citing our lack of experience in the world of widgets: "We're different. You guys may be the hotshots of high-tech industries, computing, or whatever, but my guess is your calculations are irrelevant to widgets."

McMills had touched a nerve, because in fact we had never worked with a widget company before. He had also unleashed my incurable urge to plead the case by example. Sometimes it works, sometimes not; but it was worth a try in this case. Instead of resorting to war stories that roughly approximated the world of widgets, I decided on a flanking attack. "Butch, if you think we're trying to force square pegs into round holes, then consider the sedate world of financial services. Last year, believe it or not, I called on the number-two person in an eastern insurance company. My mission there was the same as it is here. That company was and is rock solid, like the building it occupies. Stepping out on the fifth floor, I beheld a scene light years away from the one we're sitting in now: painted landscapes in gilt frames hanging on paneled walls, leather wing chairs, wall-to-wall carpet, and an atmosphere so still you could hear the ticking of the grandfather clock.

"My host, a distinguished-looking executive in his early sixties, matched the decor perfectly. I felt like a fish out of water, especially after learning that the sumptuous surroundings were not marred by any overhead projectors on which I might display my trusty charts. I handed my host a pack of printed charts and plunged into my presentation, but I soon saw that it wasn't working. I couldn't even establish eye contact. Instead I offered to field any questions.

"Eye contact at last! The executive's first question was, 'What do you know about financial services?' Nothing, I admitted. 'Well, then,' he countered, 'why are you here?'

"'Because I understand cycle time,' I told him. 'I understand white-collar productivity. I understand performance improvement. And that's 80 percent of the problem and solution in any company. You and your people have enough subject matter experience in financial services for both of us. What I know, and what you need, is all the rest.' I went on then to explain how the baseline/entitlement gap is largely a case of *generic* barriers.

"When I had finished, my host looked at me and said,

'You're about the fiftieth person who has sat in that chair trying to convince me that we should do something to change
this institution. But you're the first one who admitted he
didn't understand the business. The others didn't either, of
course, but you're the only one who could demonstrate that it
need not matter, so we're going to do business with you.'

"The point of that story is that what's good for a $20 billion
corporation may prove good enough for General Widget.
But, in case you're not persuaded yet, consider the case of a
window company we analyzed as an acquisition a while back.
That firm specialized in custom aluminum extrusion-type
windows. It handled every aspect of the operation, starting
with aluminum ingots and finishing with complex insulated
glass windows and doors in painted aluminum frames. Its total business was about $40 million annually, but it was start-
ing to lose money, and its parent company decided to sell it
off. After a quick look at the company, we decided it was a
good buy. Why? Not because any of us know word one about
the nuts and bolts of aluminum windows, but because we
could see opportunity in that operation that its own practitio-
ners had overlooked.

"Generally speaking, the aluminum-window business of-
fers growth opportunities because it's highly regionalized
and virtually free of foreign competition. Its biggest pitfall is
the instability of aluminum prices. That alone ought to pro-
mote short cycle times and minimal inventory. The opposite,
however, was the case here, as it is throughout that industry.
The company in question had developed bad habits. In fact,
all that was keeping it alive were the uniformly long cycle
times of its competition: about six weeks from order entry to
delivery.

"As part of our analysis, we did a baseline/entitlement
study and concluded that entitlement was half a day for order entry, two days for manufacturing, another half a day
for distribution: a total of several days at most, not several
weeks. The company management didn't believe we knew
what we were talking about. They gave us the old refrain,

'You guys don't know the business, and anyway, we're as fast as the competition.' Sound familiar? Well, we knew Total Cycle Time, and in view of the tremendous opportunity it represented, we decided to try to buy the company, but while we were arranging financing, the parent corporation went into Chapter Eleven and another alert buyer with cash in hand beat us out. If we had been the winning buyer, today you would be talking to an expert in aluminum extrusion window production. The bottom line here is that we don't have to be specialists in a field to see the barriers therein. And, given the chance, we're not afraid to put our own money on the line. That should speak volumes to you about our level of commitment. So, by the way, should the fact that we're working at General Widget on an incentive basis.

"The main question at hand is whether or not Total Cycle Time is *generally* applicable. Let's skip to another extreme: advanced government contracting. Just last year, a major producer of weapons systems hired us to shorten its cycle times. One of the company's biggest problems involved the purchasing of materials. Its 'dock-to-stock' procurement system was highly automated, with a colossal database, elaborate software, bar code capability—the works. Its objective, I'm happy to say, was to keep inventories at a minimum and cycle times short by scheduling the precise delivery of necessary components to the company dock. Accordingly, it operated on a Japanese-style 'just-in-time' basis, in which all deliveries were prescheduled to arrive within a predictable five-minute delivery period. Now, this was not a small task. It involved the receipt and processing of about 3000 separate items, not one of which, incidentally, was a widget. Upon arrival at a central location, electrical components, insulation material, screws, brackets, packing materials, and whatever were received, checked against the order, inspected, and forwarded to a usable manufacturing inventory. The whole process averaged 15 working days and employed about 600 people.

"The system was technically impressive, all right, but looks can be deceiving. For example, trucks did indeed back up to the dock and scoot away, but the backing and scooting wasn't necessarily just-in-time at all. In some cases, the split-second deliveries contained materials that were a month early or a month late! Imagine the concentric waves of trouble that reverberated through the system as late, early, and on-time items were matched to their purchase orders, bar-coded, age-tested and/or vulnerability-tested, mechanically tested, shake-rattle-and-roll-tested, and routed to their appropriate manufacturing area. Upon inspection, we found that little more than half the deliveries went through without some kind of hitch. In other words, the first-pass yield was about 56 percent. We determined that the process could be streamlined to about four days.

"As always, we found three categories of barriers. The first were product-oriented. These we could sometimes identify but lacked the expertise to fix, so the talent within the company took care of them without much help from us. But there were also process barriers such as redundant procedures that insiders found hard to spot. Once we had identified them, however, they were readily eliminated by the company's in-place implementation and quality teams. We were able to provide some software solutions to lubricate the process further.

"The biggest hang-ups proved to be cultural. The company's organizational structure, in place for 20 years, was unsuited to the proposed short cycle time. The process embodied the best thinking of people from several disparate fields of expertise. Each group of experts had inflicted its own pet procedures on the system. It was therefore riven with procedures which, though impressively automated, constituted a belt-and-suspenders overkill that management had difficulty seeing. It also perpetuated the different factions within the organization that were working at cross purposes. Finally and inevitably, the traditional measurements and controls in use were inadequate to the changing times. Yet these conditions were so fundamentally rooted, nobody in the company had recognized them as obstructive. It took outsiders to point out such fundamental deficiencies. With all three types of barriers overcome, the company's first-pass yield improved dramatically, its inventory was cut by $8 million, and its massive reliance on overtime was virtually eliminated. What was the cycle time? Four days, down from fifteen."

I could have gone on and on because I love to tell such stories, but the supervisors who a minute before were nodding their heads were now furtively looking at their watches. McMills, though, was still looking straight at me. Was that a nod I saw? It was time for a wrap-up.

"Remember these examples," I said. "The opportunities for performance improvement I described would never have been identified by day-to-day experts in insurance, or aluminum windows, or sophisticated weapons systems, nor would many of the barriers to entitlement. Three kinds of barriers must be eliminated. You people know more about the first type than my people ever will. You are the experts on, say, whether a widget should have a gloss finish or a matte finish. The other two areas, process and culture, are our specialties. When, where, and how often should that widget be inspected during production? How can Manufacturing better interface with Marketing? That sort of thing.

"I hope today I've made believers out of you. If not, we'll have to fall back for the moment on Mr. King's general order for compliance. In time I think you will all be believers."

In the days that followed, our team put together a customized training program that emphasized the generic as it transferred TGI skills to General Widget: how to calculate and control cycle times, for example, and how best to deploy inventory relative to throughput, process, and recovery times. Even after the training programs, however, a number of individuals failed to implement important principles. In one case, as business grew, Production Control repeatedly tried to increase inputs to the manufacturing line. That was exactly the wrong thing to do if cycle times were to decline. The consequence was a lot of expediting and a wide spread of results, with many critical orders being delivered behind schedule and too many high-priority hot lots in the operation. Faced with these problems, Manufacturing people were reluctant to take the steps necessary to reduce cycle times. Coming full circle: as output fell, Production Control tried again and again to increase input, creating a new barrier to lower cycle time. In view of the snarl, I took advantage of one of Manufacturing's crack-of-dawn meetings to restress a few fundamentals.

Stepping to the conference room blackboard one gloomy morning, I rewrote the equation that all of them had seen several times before:

$$\text{Cycle time} = \frac{\text{Work in Process (WIP)}}{\text{Speed}}$$

"Speed," I elaborated, "is determined by the marketplace. The only way speed can be changed is to increase your organization's ability to process units per hour, or to increase the number of working hours per week. In other words, you must raise yields, work longer hours, and/or improve productivity if you expect to move the line faster. Now, the ramping your line is presently undergoing is prompting you first to increase your WIP and then to fret about speeding up. Wrong! You've got to increase your capability to generate more output before raising WIP. Otherwise you will slow down your cycle time and reduce output. That is exactly what has been going on lately. Remember in ramping up, speed first, WIP second."

Expediting tardy orders by designating them as hot lots was standard procedure at General Widget, and over the years, Production Control Manager Eve Proctor had used this route so often it was now ingrained in her approach. But Manufacturing also operated by another rule that fixed the maximum of hot lots at 25 percent of the total WIP.

I wrote another equation on the board:

$$\text{WIP} = \text{Active work in process} + \text{Banked work in process}$$

"Active WIP," I continued, "is that which is on the machines and is being worked on at any point in time. Banked WIP is whatever work you keep between machines to compensate for speed differences of the machinery and the recovery time of a machine that breaks down."

We all did some calculations, placing the present level of total WIP at 12,500 units, about 2500 of which were active. (Entitlement WIP in this case was 5000.) But in reality the line was currently running hot lots to the tune of more than 3000 units, a figure that exceeded the optimum figure for active WIP. In other words, the only units moving on the line were hot lots. "No wonder your customers are shouting about the lack of delivery," I told them.

Butch McMills hardly wasted a second before speaking up. "From now on, Manufacturing will reduce the number of hot lots on the line to less than 900 widgets. In addition, we're going to reduce our input of widgets to 90 percent of the output of widgets until we've brought our inventories in line."

It was a breakthrough! I looked at Proctor, who was having trouble finding her mouth with the filter end of her cigarette. She spoke: "But I need these lots to get the kind of product mix for different customers." The mix issue unleashed a long discussion about lot sizes. Lots of fifty had been standard ever since machinery designed for that quantity had been installed. It was the old story: The lot sizes were being loaded according to the analysis of industrial engineering and the convenience of the equipment, not the needs of the customer, and the line was now swimming in inventory.

McMills asked Proctor what size orders the hot lots represented. "Well," she admitted, "in most cases 10 or 15 would get the customer out of trouble." Such a lot size would also get manufacturing out of trouble, of course, by reducing the hot-lot clutter. Hot-lot inventory would drop to a little over 600 widgets, very close to acceptable. McMills gave the order that, until further notice, hot lots would be run in 10-unit batches.

Since my days at TI, I had seen the lot-size problem in dozens of manifestations, and I thought a brief story might help McMills and his group put theirs in perspective.

"Maybe this will make you feel better," I told them. "A while back, I visited a plant within a printing and publishing company to assess performance. The preliminary data I'd received included the information that manufacturing lot size was '1.2M,' a figure that seemed to stand for 1.2 million books. 'There has to be a mistake here,' I told my hosts. 'No mistake,' they said."

"I couldn't wait to see that operation. Eventually I was ushered into an enormous, cavernous, warehouselike building with machinery to match, running full tilt. All of the presses were grouped in a central area. In another area were grouped the assembly machines. Painted on the floor around the equipment was a series of traffic lanes worthy of an interstate freeway. The freeway effect was completed by a lot of forklift trucks speedily hustling along the designated lanes and maneuvering to and from the machinery and the immense storage areas in the distance. It was a riot of noisy activity, all in the name of turning out 1.2 million books at a crack.

The reason for this production nightmare and its subsequent storage and marketing migraines, as you've probably guessed, was that the company had purchased large presses capable of such output. 'Wouldn't it be easier to reduce the lot size?' I asked. 'Many of your performance problems clearly stem from that one factor.' I was told, of course, that such quantities had been calculated by industrial engineers and 'maximized the efficiency of the presses.' At General Widget, you ought to count your blessings. Looked at from the publishing perspective, a few dozen widgets is a small headache indeed." Everybody but Eve Proctor smiled.

I was not surprised when, after the meeting, Proctor intercepted me in the hall. "I think it would be a good idea for us to talk, if you can spare the time," she said. Under the circumstances, I was glad to, for I feared that Proctor might become a major barrier to continued progress. We bought two cups of tea from a vending machine and went to her office. While it stopped short of being unpleasant, the conversation that followed did little to allay either of our anxieties.

It quickly became evident that Proctor had kept silent during the meeting because, while she did not buy our ideas, she was anxious about appearing stupid or obstructive in front of her colleagues. At her request, I delivered a one-on-one tutorial, rehashing such fundamentals as 'less in means more out' and illustrating the equations we had covered at the meeting with a few actual anecdotes. I could see that I wasn't changing her mind. When I had finished, Proctor leaned back in her chair, lit a cigarette, and blew a stream of smoke at the ceiling. "It's not as though I don't see what you're driving at," she said. "I recognize that your ideas are logical within the context of Total Cycle Time. But I can't escape the conviction that they're quite irrelevant to the real-world situations I've had to cope with here for years. If I seem nervous about the whole situation, I am."

She leaned forward and looked me straight in the eye. "Here's the real world," she continued. "I've been with General Widget 22 years. As Production Control manager, I've saved the company's bacon on many, many occasions. You might be surprised at the number of times engineering has botched up, or the manufacturing line has gone haywire, or customers have been enraged by our inability to deliver on time. On those occasions, I was the one on the spot. You seem obsessed with low inventories. I'm here to tell you that over the years, I've been able to head off quite a few crises in the making because I had the foresight to accumulate inventory, or to rush hot lots through in the nick of time. You say that Total Cycle Time requires no new investment in labor or equipment. Based upon my experience, I say that the work force and equipment we've got on hand will probably get into more trouble than usual shortening cycle times, and I don't want to be the scapegoat when that happens. The only practical way I can see to shorten cycle times is to add resources."

"What you're talking about here is security," I told her. "As you said, TCT principles don't make sense in the context you're familiar with. But that's the point. We're trying to create a new context in which these principles work. I'm talking about a new type of security. Getting high first-pass yield is security. Meeting customer demand on time is security. Beating Japanese competitors who are about to eat your lunch is security." I stopped short of adding that inasmuch as Total Cycle Time had been decreed from on high, Proctor had no choice but to get with the changes. She was only too aware of that, and it would have done no good to invoke managerial muscle. Proctor thanked me for my time and said she would take my remarks under advisement. We parted uneasily. Perhaps as things improved she would become a convert.

Every culture change includes a few good and bad surprises. With luck they even out. While Proctor might have become a barrier, her boss, Butch McMills, had gotten religion. I confirmed this by stopping in McMills's office where, surrounded by empty soft-drink cans, cigar butts, and thumbtacked family snapshots, he was scanning a printout.

McMills looked up as I entered. "The answer is yes," he said before I could speak. "I get the picture, and I'll see to it that the rest of Manufacturing goes along. By the way, I enjoy your stories. You're a little hard to stop once you're wound up, but they do make your points. Sit down a minute."

"Okay, but I'm still wound up," I replied. "When did I get through to you? Was it the story on defense contracting? Lot size?"

"Naw. You got through to me by showing you were willing to put your money where your mouth is by investing in aluminum windows! Too bad you didn't get that company. Have you bought any others?"

"Ever hear of B & B Electromatic?" I asked. He hadn't. "You'll like this quickie because it deals with your kind of problems. B & B is a nice little company in the Deep South with a niche specialty: electric barrier gates for highways, bridges, and driveways. I bought B & B from its founder-owner four years ago because I was convinced it could be a real money maker if it adopted Total Cycle Time. The company's 55-year reputation was good and so, potentially, was the president I put in place, a mechanical engineer. It goes without saying that I was not an expert in traffic barrier production.

"What followed was a case of the shoemaker's children going barefoot. As the new owner, I subjected the B & B management team to some Inspiration and Identification, provided the right measurements and controls, and left the Implementation to them. After all, I thought, a 50-person company with revenues of a million and a quarter a year should easily make the cultural change.

"Was I wrong! As soon as I was out of sight, B & B reverted to its old, comfortable way of doing things. I tried again and again. After two years, seeing no reduction in cycle time or inventory, I lowered the boom. I drove to B & B, closed the conference room door behind me, and proceeded to read the president the riot act. The company, I told him in loud tones, was supposed to grow. It was supposed to throw off cash, not consume it. I gave him a graphic lecture on Total Cycle Time culture and ended simply by demanding shorter cycle times, better customer response, lower inventory, and smaller lot sizes. Then I stormed out.

"That apparently did the trick. The president summoned his subordinates, saying he had just suffered the worst three hours of his career and that he was about to spread the unpleasantness around. Things started to improve thereafter and have continued that way for two years. I estimate that this year's profits will be close to the company's gross revenues before Total Cycle Time.

"Why did the turnaround take so long? I found out that for two years, the B & B people thought they were saving me from myself because I knew nothing about the traffic barrier business. Consequently, the inventory remained out of sight. Because their machinery had the capability, they were producing gears in lots of 100 when 25 would have filled immediate orders. While, admittedly, they made an eventual saving on setup time, they meanwhile had to pay out the cash to carry 75 gears we didn't need. Under pressure, they cut the lot size to 25. Now they're thinking of dropping to 12. By the same token, when one of their in-service machines broke down, which necessitated supplying one standard spare part, the company, in its wisdom, decided to 'optimize the utilization of its machine tools' by producing a lot of 20. That, they believed, was the 'economical' way to produce parts. They shipped one part out and put 19 into inventory. Those soon became a write-off. With the cost of borrowing money today, if you produce 20 parts to get 1, you've eaten up the full cost of the 1 in interest on the other 19 in half a year. That's the sort of room for improvement that had prompted me to buy the company. I'm only chagrined that it took as long as it did to achieve the right results. Anyway, B & B's work force has dropped by about a third, and its sales have more than doubled. We're looking to increase the business to over $5 million in the next few years at well over 30 percent pretax.

"Now, would you like me to share any other experiences with you?"

McMills looked at me to see if I·was kidding. I wasn't. "That would be interesting," he said, "but it's past my bedtime."

Barriers: The Second Wave

Over the ensuing months, we expanded our previous analysis of historical data, theoretical cycle time, and the barriers to cycle time reduction in Manufacturing. Data revealed that several parts of the manufacturing line had rushed high-priority units through at speeds lower than our estimates for entitlement. When training exercises and data analysis were shared, both the supervisors and our team concluded that 16 days was perhaps too conservative an estimate for Manufacturing. The next step was to get Manufacturing personnel to accept the truth that the line could operate every day with the dispatch it had displayed on a few rare occasions.

Meanwhile, the time had dropped to 27 days; then it stalled. In the hall and at the coffee machines, we picked up the rumor that the TGI calculations were off and that 27 days was, in fact, entitlement, because at that point, the cycle time just would not budge. Several weeks went by without any progress. Then the cycle time began to edge ominously upward.

As soon as our measurements had revealed the stall, a team was dispatched to the manufacturing floor to identify the new barrier. At last we found it, in the manner supervisors were reporting the downtime and recovery of machinery. If, for example, a machine went down on the second or third shift, it was not repaired until the next first shift, because that was where the maintenance people were primarily deployed. Thus, a machine that went down at 10 p.m. and was fixed by noon the next day would appear in the data to have been down only 3 hours, not 14. McMills quickly redeployed his maintenance crews equally among the shifts.

We also readdressed the problem of lot sizes which, experience shows, are almost invariably a factor in reducing make/market cycle time. General Widget was operating with lot sizes as high as 200, although 50 was usual. These sizes had been prescribed by industrial engineers as "economical," given the capacities of the equipment. Fortunately, Prudence Cash's recent quantification of other factors permitted us to examine the question from the point of view of the customer, taking into account the impacts of carrying cost, obsolescence, customer response, market share, and, of course, proper utilization of equipment. Our first step was to reduce the large lot sizes from 200 to 50. Once the line grew comfortable with that number and cycle time declined accordingly, we convinced Manufacturing to cut lot sizes to 25.

At that point, engineers predicted all kinds of gloom and doom. Wouldn't running so many small lots overwhelm the computers that tracked lot movement on the line? No. We explained that if the cycle time was cut by half, computers would be tracking the same number of lots. We cut the lot sizes and waited for weeks until Manufacturing people again grew comfortable with small numbers. When they had accepted the principle that small lots improve cycle times, we pushed to reduce the average size to 10.

There was more resistance. This time, the argument was that so many small lots required a substantial increase in setup time. We were asked to revise our figures for theoretical cycle time to include the increased number of setups. This we declined to do. Setup time is not included in theoretical calculations, and setup time had already been taken into account in determining the multiple of theoretical that constituted entitlement. It would be General Widget's task to reduce setup cycle times just as it had done in the case of reducing equipment recovery times, inasmuch as the two are identical in their impact.

When Manufacturing's cycle time dropped to just below 20 days and we could almost taste entitlement, we hit another barrier. Several manufacturing people insisted that the line was now truly running at entitlement, and once again they worried that there must be something wrong with our calculations. Much to our chagrin, it turned out we had indeed made a mistake: Our calculations of process flow had omitted an entire manufacturing step.

Here is the story: Several years before, General Widget had discovered that humid conditions in the manufacturing area were affecting quality. Consequently, an off-line oven had been set up in an uncrowded but distant spot within the building. Widgets were moved in lots off the line to this oven, baked in two 48-hour stages, and returned to the line for completion. Two years later, when it upgraded its facility, General Widget had eliminated the humidity problem, but somehow nobody thought to eliminate the baking step. We didn't see the ovens during our inspection of the line. Consequently our estimate of entitlement did not include the time it took for that pointless baking step. The engineers saw the light and baking was immediately eliminated, after which, sure enough, the line indeed ran close to its entitlement. In the bargain, floor space, transportation, and electrical costs were also freed up. (Incidentally, the episode points up vividly the need for eyeball inspection of every step in every process in every nook and cranny.)

It took awhile for the domino to strike Hunter Meritt, General Widget's quality director. During our first month at General Widget, when we seemed to be up against a stone wall in Manufacturing, Meritt had sought me out to safeguard his quality program. Clearly, he thought himself and his program jeopardized by our presence. He began our conversation by stating his dedication to the newly popular concept of total quality, which espoused a meticulous and permanent commitment to quality improvement in every facet of a business. But, he said, he had been frustrated in trying to implement such a program across the company.

At General Widget, as elsewhere, quality had become more than a motherhood issue. Meritt had convinced both King and Prince that improving quality would directly increase the company's profitability.

"They understood that good quality is good business and that it more than pays for itself," Meritt told me, "but they couldn't decide which direction to take to exploit quality improvement. We perceived two strategic alternatives. If our quality program reduced costs and waste, we could cut our prices and regain market share. On the other hand, we could go for broke and achieve a quality level that is the highest in the entire field. Premium quality would improve our customers' satisfaction, and we could charge accordingly. But because these two seemed mutually exclusive, we lost a lot of time dithering over the choice. As you know, time is something we can't spare; and all that dithering delayed our implementation of improved quality, which accordingly has become an unsexy issue in the company, although everyone pays it lip service. We go through the motions, fixing here, pep-talking there, but we're a long way from the proper culture change. In other words, our rate of improvement of total quality is far below our expectations.

"I appreciate your point that Total Cycle Time is nothing less than a change of culture, because that's what I've been saying we need for total quality. But now that you're on the scene, I'm afraid that my program will get lost in the shuffle. If I had my way, General Widget would have undertaken a total quality program instead of Total Cycle Time, because I think quality is going to be forgotten. How about it?"

This was a tough one. I knew that Total Cycle Time was exactly what Meritt needed to propel his program, but I realized that he would have to see results before he believed me. Meritt, moreover, was suffering morale problems. He probably regarded his quality directorship as a consolation prize given to him after he had been passed over for promotion, so he may have underestimated his bosses' commitment. In any case, Meritt had a bit of cultural changing to do on his own. I told him so.

"Do we perhaps suffer from a semantics problem?" I asked. "What you call 'quality,' I call cycle time and first-pass yield. No matter. You can surely see that Total Cycle Time removes barriers to better production. It gives you more Cycles of Learning with which to improve even more. It also eliminates the tie-ups in response to customers and cuts waste and costs in the process. All of those items will drive your quality program. The disciplines and controls you need for short cycle time are exactly the same as those required to realize high quality.

"As for the company's managerial confusion, quality decisions are hard to make because management is still using the old, inadequate indices and measurements of performance. That's a cultural blind spot that Total Cycle Time will overcome. Incidentally, I see no contradiction between the two strategic alternatives you outlined. Improve your cycle time and your first-pass yield and you can have leadership quality *and* cut prices if you have to. Improve your R&D responsiveness and you can beat the competition to the marketplace with first-rate, high-quality innovations that set their own price. When that happens, you'll have no trouble selling top management on total quality because you will have arrived at total quality. And I'm sure you appreciate that the potential for continuous quality improvement keeps spiraling upward as a company reaches entitlement and utilizes its increased Cycles of Learning."

We let things go at that. But shortly afterward, when Manufacturing's cycle time started to shorten, Meritt began to note reduced numbers of reworks. Seeing was believing, he said. We ceased to be a threat in his mind.

Meritt nonetheless pointed out that General Widget's overall quality, while improving, was still inferior to the Japanese competition's, despite the fact that yield figures ran better than 90 percent. Why? The answer was that we used a different quality yardstick than overall yield, because that figure hid a substantial number of reworks. Using first-pass yield as the criterion, we came up with a figure of only 72 percent.

Manufacturing's Sustaining Engineering Group, under Manny Bolster, was responsible for implementing quality improvement, but our yield figures showed that Sustaining Engineering was not utilizing its increased Cycles of Learning to proper advantage. Prince, Meritt, and I sat down with Bolster, who told us he was understaffed for such a responsibility. Rather than helping the problem-solving team, Bolster's hard-pressed engineers had all they could do to manage the circumstantial problems that arose during manufacturing. Bolster, however, understood Cycles of Learning, having taken the training program we had lately presented.

"Get me three more guys and train them, and I'll develop an effective feedback loop," he told Prince. He got them. TGI adapted one of its prior training programs to General Widget's specific needs, including exercises in high-low diagnostics and the use of statistical and analytical techniques to isolate yield-constraining mechanisms. The training involved five 4-hour sessions, not including homework.

After 15 months, first-pass yield was at 90 percent and Meritt was ecstatic. So, by then, were Prince and McMills, because the impact of Cycles of Learning had reduced rework and improved the utilization of equipment.

Meanwhile, Manufacturing's planning cycle time was shortened. At baseline, it had operated by the month, using last month's data to load the line for the month to come. With imposition of first-in, first-out discipline on the line, reduction of the need to expedite hot lots, and simplification of some of the review material, it became possible to plan on a weekly basis without adding any planning resources, a change that cut the make/market cycle by 14 days.

A Turn for the Worse?

One of the more interesting personal stories at General Widget was the gradual change in attitude of Victor King. At the outset, remember, King had hoped to achieve buy-in and had also been wary of getting the company too deeply involved financially in the effort to reach entitlement—hence his choice to engage us primarily on an incentive basis. Once the program was under way, however, he gave us all the support we asked for, exerting his personal authority as needed. I couldn't help noticing that we almost always had to ask for it, however. He seemed naturally predisposed to keep his distance—a stance that fitted his unflappably cool deportment.

Almost a year into the process, when Total Cycle Time was no longer moot among his managers, he contacted me, asking pointedly if I did not agree with him that the culture change was in place and that General Widget could manage its own progress from that point on. Not only did I disagree, but I took his request as evidence that King had not fully adjusted on his own to the culture change.

Superficially, it probably looked to King as though Total Cycle Time was self-propelled. As CEO, he had personally witnessed dramatic changes in the use of his own time. For-

merly, he told me, he had devoted hours of each week to customer relations, by which he meant listening to and personally interceding on behalf of complaining customers. As cycle
times shortened, he had had fewer and fewer of these
chores, but his time had been preempted by another distraction: listening to and mediating the displeasure of subordinates who were feeling the discomfort of changing times. To
his credit, King faced down managerial complaints in the
general interest. Sure enough, when General Widget began
to reap the payoffs of Total Cycle Time, complaints tapered
off, leaving the CEO more time than he had had in years to
strategize. That, to him, was a signal that the culture change
had been institutionalized.

About a month after the above contact, he changed his
tune because it looked from his vantage point as though his
company was again in trouble. I learned this, not from King
himself, but from Sellers, who nervously corralled me for an
emergency meeting with the CEO late one Friday afternoon.
"We've got problems," Sellers said as we headed for King's
beige-on-beige inner sanctum.

Both King and Sellers used horn-rimmed reading glasses
while at work, the half-lens kind that are worn well down the
bridge of the nose. At serious moments, King would sit back
in his chair, interlace his fingers under his chin and, otherwise motionless, affix you with an expressionless but unset-
tling gaze over the tops of his glasses. The pose was known
around the office as the King Ray, and when you felt it, you
knew you were expected to come up with something fast.
Sellers, by contrast, used his glasses largely as a prop at such
times, taking them on and off and waving them about to emphasize his points. That afternoon in King's office, there was
a good deal of gazing and waving.

"As you know, Hardy, I called you in here to explain to me
why our orders are down," King began. Turning to me, he
added, "You're here to explain why they're not up, in view of
our declining cycle times." As soon as Sellers began to pace,
wave, and talk, I realized what had happened and kicked myself for not warning Sellers in advance.

Sellers began: "When you asked me about this informally last week, I didn't have a clue. Now I think I understand it, but I'm still nervous. It does indeed relate to Total Cycle Time. As Philip here can attest, Marketing has played the entitlement game well, and I haven't let grass grow under my feet, either. As soon as I saw that shorter cycle times would give us better customer response, I put together a dog-and-pony show that I personally presented to our top seven accounts. My sales managers handled the remainder. In this presentation, I outlined General Widget's progress toward entitlement (although I did not use that term). I also described in detail the improvements in response we were now capable of, and I frankly asked for a bigger share of their market, based upon our superior ability in customer service. The presentations went beautifully, and I was congratulated everywhere I went. After I got home from my swing around the country, I even celebrated by taking my wife to the country club for dinner. I even remember gloating a little over champagne and telling Suzy that the company was in for a business surge.

"What followed confirms the old saw that no good deed goes unpunished. Almost immediately after that, our key customers started reducing their orders! That was three months ago, and things have been skidding ever since. At first I thought it was some sort of market glitch, but six weeks ago I told my regional managers to get us some customer feedback. The purchasing agents they deal with were friendly and full of praise for General Widget, but they did not place orders.

"I decided to find out for myself, so I personally contacted the seven companies I had visited. Here's the gist of what they said: 'Of course we intend to reorder from you.' Two customers even said they'd probably increase their orders. 'We simply don't need any more at the moment. Your supply times used to be so long that we had to keep 16 weeks of inventory around. Now you're down to 6 weeks, so we're using up the stuff we already bought and paid for.' In other words, things will change, but with falling cycle time, they're going to get a little worse before they get better. I think we should take the dip in orders as a kind of compliment, although I can do without such compliments."

The King Ray turned upon me. "It is a compliment," I said. "I've seen this phenomenon dozens of times. It's a temporary side effect of progress. It was a serious oversight on my part not to alert General Widget about it in advance, and I apologize. But orders will revive within a matter of weeks. I promise." We agreed to meet again as soon as orders revived.

Meanwhile, momentary withholding of orders by General Widget's prime customers precipitated one of the most unpleasant episodes in the two-year march to entitlement. At the time the company's manufacturing productivity and yield had increased output by 20 percent, its business had grown by only 10 percent. Even after the elimination of most overtime, it looked as though layoffs were in the offing, which, as King himself told me, was the dirtiest trick anyone could play on a motivated work force.

There was no doubt that for a while, layoffs were inevitable. Manufacturing ran on three shifts, and Prince contended that the entire third shift should be eliminated to maintain the productive integrity of the two that remained. I successfully pushed for equal cutbacks in all three shifts to maintain the integrity of the shortening cycle times. Union considerations, however, required McMills to consider seniority at layoff times. Consequently, when the cutback came, the inevitable shuffling of seasoned workers from shift to shift and job to job created a subset of headaches.

Rumors about probable layoffs were already afoot, so we decided to defuse the bombshell as best we could with a full explanation. The first step was to meet with union officials, local and national. As hoped, the presence of the latter helped cool some of the anger of the former. I had a bet with Prince about what the first question would be. My money was on "Are you people going to close the plant?" Prince was betting on "Are you people going out of business?" and he won.

We had a long way to go, in that meeting, from those apprehensions to the assurances we wanted to give that the layoff would be quite temporary. We took advantage of the occasion to pump in as much short-cycle-time thinking as possible.

After hearing the rationale, the union leadership was resigned to the layoff and amenable to the tactic of keeping all three shifts active to continue the cycle time changes, so long as seniority was observed. The next task was to give the news to the work force in as constructive a way as possible.

Prince prepared a shift-by-shift presentation to General Widget's direct-labor people. In his talk, which was backed up by published handouts, he explained the three-shift layoff rationale. Needless to say, it went over more smoothly in the third shift period than the other two. In every case, however, the news brought rumblings from the floor, punctuated by shouts of "Why?"

Prince told them why. Because the work force had already been exposed to short cycle time thinking, he could concentrate on the tactical situation. Accordingly, he identified Japan as General Widget's chief threat. He actually used the word *threat*, because he wanted his work force to view Japanese workers as competition and abandon any notion that their own union was a security blanket in a changing world. The only security, Prince emphasized, was better performance. Prince stipulated that American workers were the equal of Japan's. He was then joined by McMills, who said he could prove it. McMills identified short cycle time as the key to competitive performance, pointedly adding that reductions in work force would be temporary if the effort continued. These words sounded a lot more dramatic than they were, because it was only a matter of time before sales overtook capacity.

But the issue of overseas competition raised inevitable and sharp questions about General Widget's own offshore facility. Prince was ready for these. "Before we began the move to Total Cycle Time," he told one shift, "I was under considerable pressure to allocate more and more of our production to Kaohsiung. But some interesting things have happened over the last year that I want to share with you all. As you probably know, we have found it profitable to make our transfer prices to the Taiwan plant very low, sell our products out of Taiwan, and leave the profit there in a tax haven."

Hearing mutterings and seeing shrugs, Prince provided a brief explanation of how the tax haven worked. "The period for that tax haven has now expired," he continued. "With the new U.S. tax rates and our gains in domestic productivity, the arguments for sending more General Widget production offshore have also expired. We've come to the point where the best place to make a profit is right here. In fact, Butch McMills tells me we can now manufacture the line of products we were planning to transfer to Taiwan right here. That will be management's commitment to improving competitiveness. We ask that you match that commitment by helping us through a short period of cutbacks until our business catches up with our strengthened capacity."

The handling of the touchy layoff went about as well as could be expected, although it was harder in some ways on McMills than others. On his way back to his office after the last of his stirring speeches, he was lured into a shoving and shouting match with a long-time worker whose anger made it clear we would never see him again. And, as we walked across the parking lot to head for home, McMills noticed that his Bronco was about six inches lower than usual. All four tires were flat. He reddened a little, then said, "Could be worse. At least they left the windshield this time. Come on. I'll swap you a beer for a ride home."

During the 12-week layoff, we admonished supervisors to keep a close watch on inventory. Many workers, for whom high inventory levels represented security, had falsely perceived a connection between the reduction in inventory and the cutbacks in the work force. They were bound to work at a slower pace than before, hoping to drive up inventory to their baseline comfort levels. Every supervisor on every shift was going to have to ram home the point that security now lay in competitiveness, not inventory backlog.

Three months after the layoffs, it was suddenly time to re-hire. General Widget's chief customers came through with the expected orders, and new business was continuing to rise. The returnees, phased back in according to seniority, were carefully monitored by supervisors so that the old, inventory-heavy practices did not return. Six weeks after the upturn, all the laid-off employees had been called back to work and the company was in overtime.

Unfortunately, the ramp in production was mismanaged by Production Control. When orders began to mount, Eve Proctor had increased the operating plan, scheduling a higher input rate. As a result, WIP inventory and cycle times went up. Proctor was acting out of experience and a gut re-action that impelled her to increase input in order to get more output. Doing so was, of course, contrary to our advice and Prince's general instructions. Convinced that she was right, she flatly refused to cut inputs. Proctor had made her-self a barrier.

How to remove such a barrier was a question that caused Prince, McMills, and me to burn the midnight oil on two suc-cessive evenings. Prince at last resolved to replace her, but wanted to move her aside in a way that dignified her years of service and, if possible, relocate her to a spot where her ex-perience might still be useful.

Proctor's designated replacement was a relative newcomer and subordinate who, with a little shadow management, would surely fit into the new culture. It was certain that Proc-tor would not accept a position in Production Control work-ing for a former assistant. When confidentially apprised of the situation, L. J. Byer offered to fit her into a responsible but subordinate position in Purchasing. The other alterna-tive, inasmuch as Proctor was in her early fifties, was early retirement. After a private meeting with Prince, who ex-plained her options to her, Proctor elected early retirement.

Breathing Easier

As agreed several weeks before, Sellers and I met in King's office to review the company's changed circumstances. This time around, the atmosphere was inevitably more pleasant, and Sellers could hardly wait to begin.

"Listen to this. Three days ago I got a call from one of my area managers. He was really excited. He had just closed a piece of business that had previously belonged to a Japanese company, and the reason for getting this business was our ability to respond to the customer's need in a shorter time than the competition. The next day, my phone rang again. This time it was another regional manager, saying that we'd won a new contract because the customer needed widgets in a hurry and we were the only house that could supply them on time. We didn't even have to quibble about price. It was obvious that our speed was worth paying a premium for. I'd say we're out of the doldrums." He was right.

Hands Across the Sea

General Widget's Taiwan plant, which reported directly to Prince, had been placed low on our rank-ordered list of priorities, in view of the work to be done in Philadelphia. As Implementation began to yield domestic results, Prince wanted to know when and where the offshore facility fitted into the new culture.

"How can we quickly extend cycle time know-how to Kaohsiung?" he asked. "Could we send them a presentation and a how-to manual? I'm sure, once they got the message, they would apply themselves to the new culture with real ardor."

I replied that things were not so easy or so cheap. Kaohsiung should receive the same outside assessment that Philadelphia had, for the same reasons. I recommended that he and I go to Taiwan and do an on-the-spot baseline and entitlement analysis together, simultaneously starting the Inspiration and Identification phases. Those chores should take a week.

A second week would be required to start the Information (training) and Implementation phases. It was essential that the Operations VP personally launch the program, itemizing its effects in Philadelphia and making it clear that commensurate impacts are expected in Kaohsiung. Then, we both should plan to spend one week every two months for a year on-site, acting as coaches and catalysts.

It took a while to schedule the first trip. Prince was in no mood for such a distraction, and judging from the numerous telexes that poured in from Taiwan, neither was his offshore manager, X. Pat Farr. Farr had made it clear to Prince that things were fine in Kaohsiung and that no visits, ceremonial or otherwise, would be required to get his people off and running toward Total Cycle Time.

"That's typical," admitted Prince. "Pat Farr is one of those seasoned Far East hands who loves it over there, speaks the languages, and hardly ever comes home. He's been running our Taiwan operation since 1969, and the less he hears from the home office, the better he likes it."

Exactly four weeks after Prince and I made our Far East plans, we landed in Taipei and flew down to Kaohsiung. We were met at the airport by Pat Farr, a confident, good-humored manager built along the lines of Butch McMills but with a more relaxed manner. As our car (a very large, very clean black Chrysler that lumbered like a tank in Kaohsiung's congested traffic) rolled up to the two-story cement-block plant over which Farr presided, a pair of photographers ran alongside snapping pictures. I had underestimated the momentousness of the visit, and so had Prince, who told me as the car slowed to a stop that this was the first time a senior stateside executive of General Widget had set foot in the plant since the day it was officially dedicated. His voice was drowned out by the clatter of exploding firecrackers thrown in the car's path. On each side of the driveway, lined up like fenceposts and wearing big smiles, was the plant's entire work force. Over the main entrance to the building was draped a banner reading: "WELCOME VICE PRESIDENT PRINCE."

Vice President Prince and I got right to work, establishing the assembly plant's baseline and theoretical cycle times, including transit times, vendor cycle times, manufacturing, production control and administration of incoming and outgoing lots, packing, shipping, customs, and other paperwork. After we computed entitlement, we expected the usual resistance, but to our surprise, Farr and his subordinates seemed enthusiastic and eager to get started. Farr's only comment was that, based upon his contacts with other expatriates in the "old boy network," his plant's cycle times were as short or shorter than any in Taiwan, Singapore, Hong Kong, or South Korea. I wondered, then, what prompted his amenability. Like many hands in the Far East, he had perhaps learned when it was necessary to unquestioningly accept orders from City Hall. Or was it that he saw an opportunity that his competitors did not have?

By the end of the first week, training programs were under way and everyone seemed to take to the new system. When we departed, we took Farr with us to Philadelphia for training and allowed ourselves to hope that the Taiwan plant would make a relatively easy migration from its baseline to entitlement. But our training had underemphasized the fact that there would be new barriers to overcome as cycle time plummeted.

It was not long before Prince was on the business end of a stream of telexes from Taiwan, the gist of which was that the plant had achieved entitlement, although at a point much different from our projections. Impossible, replied Prince. Farr answered that our calculations must be off; Kaohsiung was at rock bottom on cycle time. Actually, Kaohsiung was on the rocks of its first series of unidentified barriers.

Prince and I had failed to appreciate the importance of the fact that, aside from Farr, the Kaohsiung plant's entire management was Taiwanese, accustomed to production-oriented criteria. Now all of that was changing. The fretful communications crossing the Pacific revealed a classic case of fear of failure and attendant loss of face. Prince and I returned to Taiwan as soon as possible to revise the program in light of this problem. Obviously, some of our procedures would need to be modified.

Back in Kaohsiung, assisted by a TGI associate whose experience in the Far East had made him fluent in Chinese, we revamped the measurements of the team. Actually, we developed a second set of measurements which expressed the objective in terms of overall productivity, time saved, yield improvements, and inventory levels reduced within the operation. The original set of procedures was confidentially given to Farr to implement. Prince made it clear that the success of the program was Farr's responsibility. That, Farr told us, would eliminate the issue of saving face among his subordinates.

Although we did not say so outright, we were prepared to tolerate considerable flexibility about the means employed at Kaohsiung to achieve entitlement: use of overtime, for example, or expenditures for new equipment. Getting short cycle times down quickly was vital to the company's overall timetable, and we were willing to return later to create the feedback loops to exploit Cycles of Learning.

Over the next year, with intermittent leadership from Prince and our team, the Kaohsiung plant's move toward entitlement appeared to be by far the smoothest of any element in General Widget. For one thing, the offshore component was isolated from the complex, interactive design, marketing, and, for the most part, manufacturing problems that characterized the stateside parent's progress. We, of course, knew that along the way, there had been many minor setbacks, which were swallowed up by the customized reporting procedures designed for Kaohsiung. Repositioning of inventory on the line and weaning managers from their voracious appetite for paperwork and multiple sign-offs proved especially

difficult. And it should be remembered that because
Kaohsiung's baseline cycle times were short to begin with,
reaching entitlement was less of a trek.

As Taiwan made progress toward its goal, Prince punctuated the key steps along the way with a scrupulous flow of
congratulatory telexes acknowledging the progress made and
the noteworthy job of all managers concerned. When the
plant neared its entitlement and its inventories were reduced
accordingly, Prince flew to Kaohsiung to officiate at an elaborate executive dinner, at which plaques and scrolls were cer-
emoniously awarded in recognition of the successful effort.
The awards were unprecedented in the plant's history, but it
was clear that they appropriately dignified a difficult and tri-
umphant struggle. Farr, who had come up with the idea, assured Prince that the trophies would soon be hanging con-
spicuously in the office of every recipient. He and Prince
decided to make the awards dinner a regular annual practice.

Selling a Vendor on Short Cycle Times

Within a year, General Widget had substantially improved its
make/market cycle time, bringing it down from 110 workdays to 55. Throughout the organization, blue- and white-
collar people were energetically using Cycles of Learning
they had created and were finding that their costs were declining rapidly. In both Philadelphia and Kaohsiung, productivity had improved by at least 20 percent. In some sales sectors,
it had improved 40 percent. The make/market goal was 45
days.

About that time, however, a problem that had been under
our noses all along was brought to our attention. It happened
at a meeting during which all parties were congratulating
themselves on the likelihood that the company would reach
its specified entitlement on schedule. Amidst the pleasant
ambience, up spoke L. J. Byer of Purchasing, who had here-
tofore said not a word.

"It's well and good to talk about all the progress we're making, but I still have to purchase A-Dads from Amalgamated for every widget we manufacture. Last year, we had to order A-Dads nine months in advance to have any certainty of delivery, and that was without change orders. In other words, we did a lot of guesswork. That was a real headache for us at baseline, but we could live with it because, frankly, we were in the same boat. But can we live with this at entitlement?"

Somehow, the A-Dad problem had escaped everyone's notice until Byer's question came up. No doubt about it, in the Total Cycle Time context, Amalgamated's problem was General Widget's problem. Within two days, Prince was on a plane to Houston, home of the A-Dad, to build a fire under Amalgamated's president, Fred Slack.

At their meeting, Slack said he was gratified by Prince's scrupulous acknowledgment that Amalgamated was crucial to General Widget's success. He added that he'd be delighted to participate in the anticipated surge Total Cycle Time was going to give to the widget business. But it was obvious that he did not know what he was committing his company to do. Prince laid it on the line: Amalgamated would have to bring its cycle times in line with General Widget's, or both companies would be in trouble. ("Deep yogurt" was the phrase Prince said he had used.)

After a quick rundown on baseline and entitlement, Prince proposed to Slack that General Widget pay for us to assess Amalgamated's baseline and entitlement. Prince made it clear that General Widget sought no unfair leverage, stressing that proprietary data provided for the study would remain strictly between Amalgamated and TGI. The details of the report would likewise be confidential. Only the final entitlement figure, which was a critical factor in General Widget's own strategy, would be revealed in Philadelphia. After that, Prince said, Amalgamated could work out the same kind of incentive arrangement as General Widget to bring the company's cycle times to entitlement.

Slack needed a couple of weeks to sort out his mixed reactions. He must have felt pressured by Prince, whose anxious

references to Amalgamated's nine-month cycle times were
unflattering. On the other hand, how could he lose? And if
the widget market picked up, he might even have a crack at
supplying A-Dads to competing firms such as WidgeCorp or
Newidget. Slack agreed to the study.

This scenario is not about Amalgamated Doodad's rush to
entitlement. Suffice it to say that the company's small size,
single specialty, and centralized location made it compara-
tively simple to assess. Amalgamated was a small company,
but not by choice. Like many vendors, its internal problems
resembled those of its end-user customers. Overall quality
was high, though rework was a problem. Until lately, it had
been able to supply orders by storing enough just-in-case inventory to meet customer demand. Requests for custom
work took forever. The company was low on cash. Its proprietary technology that had been its saving grace was now
threatened by foreign competition.

We estimated Amalgamated's entitlement as less than six
weeks; getting there would take about nine months. Slack
was surprised at this entitlement assessment, but he accepted
the incentive proposal. Amalgamated was in for a very interesting nine months. Meanwhile, General Widget had the assurance that its own projected cycle time would not be jeopardized. The incident was a sobering reminder of how Total
Cycle Time is more than an internal process. Its loops often
mesh with those in other companies, creating a therapeutic
ripple effect.

Just after Amalgamated signed on for Total Cycle Time,
Prudence Cash made an insightful suggestion regarding
Amalgamated during a progress review meeting in Philadelphia. Cash had an interesting way of twiddling her pencil
every time she got a good idea, and the pencil was atwiddle
now.

"Although Amalgamated was an accident waiting to
happen," she said, "L. J. Byer tells me that they've never let
us down. Right now they need an incentive to keep things
that way. Why don't we notify them that from now on, we'll

pay in advance for A-Dads? We can afford it and we can use
the goodwill. Amalgamated can probably use the cash. I'll see
to it that the checks are cut in Finance and go out with each
order. We'll save time, and I'll bet it gets Fred Slack's attention at the other end." Cash was getting to be an innovative
problem solver. Her idea got an immediate nod. In Houston,
every one of General Widget's subsequent orders got Fred
Slack's immediate attention.

Revolutionary War Stories

Victor King's taste in restaurants ran to the historical: stone
or brick taverns equipped with beamed ceilings, antique fur-
niture, and flintlock muskets hung over the fireplace. There
seemed to be no end of these in and around Philadelphia, although it struck me that the quality of their food was in-
versely proportional to their authenticity.

Since the night we discussed meat packing cycle times,
King and I had had several dinners together, mixing business and pleasure by the light of colonial candlesticks; or
rather, on those occasions, *he* mixed business and pleasure,
because for me there is very little difference. I find it absolutely recreational, on or off the job, to hash over the fine
points of what I do. And on our evenings together, King always let me hold forth, despite the incongruous, George-
Washington-ate-here surroundings.

On one such night, King brought up General Widget's Research and Development division: "I'm worried. I know my
development VP, Witt Tinker, sees the conceptual value of
short cycle times, but I frankly doubt if he can penetrate the
mind-set of his team. Research-oriented people have a mental block against manufacturing-based work concepts, don't
they?"

"Yes," I replied, "and it's twofold. In the first place, although they might not admit it, R&D people are often prej-
udiced against anything that smacks of the mundane, blue-

collar world. To them, there's something demeaning about fine-tuning their operation the way manufacturing types have to do. In the second place, they honestly believe that their creativity will be stifled by what looks to them like regimentation. The problem is especially close to me personally, because of the recent tribulations of one of our affiliated companies, BehaviorTech.

"In August 1985, we purchased the assets of Behavior-Tech, then a struggling consulting firm of three University of Kansas graduate students. Although the consulting part of the business had never been profitable, the students did have one very good idea. They wanted to develop and market an advanced form of computer-based training using behavioral science and artificial intelligence. Our objective was to exploit recent insights into how people learn and to produce training packages that would speed up learning and increase retention. This sort of work is primarily custom. When a client needed a high-powered training program, BehaviorTech was contracted to generate individualized packages for that purpose. The customer would provide an expert in the subject matter, and BehaviorTech would assemble the proper facts and data, storyboard the course, devise the appropriate questions to insure rapid, effective learning, and produce the necessary computer disks and materials.

"Well, as I told you, the company was populated by a small group of technical whiz kids whose abilities gave a new definition to 'white collar.' In the classic pattern of high-tech startups, we moved them into new offices and prepared to turn them loose. We told them short cycle time is good and that quality and short cycle time go hand in hand. The BehaviorTech team, however, focused on what they knew—academic excellence—which for them translated only into quality. The cycle time corollary was forgotten. They built all sorts of quality-assurance steps into their procedures. As a result, too much time was needed to deliver a course that satisfied the customer. And because the name of any custom development game is speed and cost, their approach was costing them business."

"Wait a minute," King interjected. "These guys—your guys—were right under your noses and didn't understand cycle time theory?"

"Don't rub it in. It happened because, lacking expertise in BehaviorTech's specialty, we at first gave them the benefit of the doubt, until it became obvious they needed our expertise. We demanded better performance and were greeted with the inevitable denials. We were told that the rarefied field of accelerated learning was exempt from our cycle time methodologies. Another objection was that they operated a custom shop, so each contract had its own peculiar set of problems and requirements. Finally, these people simply rejected the idea that manufacturing know-how applied to their business.

"Well, it was hard to argue back effectively because the field was brand new and had no historical record from which to calculate baseline and entitlement. But we were determined to improve performance. To overcome our lack of understanding of BehaviorTech's process, we assigned BehaviorTech the task of developing a training program on Total Cycle Time. That gave us a firsthand look into their process.

"The first thing we noted was that these people defined lot size according to the course structure. Topics defined lot sizes, not cycle times. In other words, when they contracted to provide, say, a six-hour computer-based training course, they developed the entire package in two or three lots before getting subject-matter feedback from the customer. If, as often happened, the customer didn't like what they'd done, they'd start all over from scratch and redesign the course topics (lots). If it still didn't satisfy, they did it again. To us, that translated into poor first-pass yield—or even poor second-pass yield!

"When we pointed out the inefficiency of their approach, they redefined their lot size down to one hour of computer-based training, subdividing each hour into three 20-minute modules regardless of topic size. That was a step in the right direction, although it involved too much internal checking—'quality control'—that complicated the process.

"By interacting with BehaviorTech on our own Total Cycle Time course, we demonstrated to them the benefits of customer interaction in every account. We also taught them the importance of Cycles of Learning and feedback loops. Based on our process-flow analysis, we defined a lot size as one 20-minute module of instruction. Then we ordered a module a day and applied brute force. To meet this 'customer demand,' BehaviorTech's people at first had to work literally night and day. Every morning, someone from BehaviorTech would stagger into our offices and wearily plop a module disk on our desk. That same day, we would give them material for tomorrow's module and review the latest Cycle of Learning. Needless to say, generic manufacturing-based thinking was exactly what BehaviorTech needed, and inevitably, Cycles of Learning soon did the trick. In 1987, BehaviorTech was doing about $500 thousand in business. In 1988 the figure jumped to over $1 million. It more than doubled the next year, and we expect to do about $20 million in the early to mid-90s.

"Impressive," King admitted, "but I know what the people in General Widget's R&D division would say to that story. You were, after all, working with brand-new material, and captives at that."

"Well then," I answered, "I'd just have to give them a more pertinent example, such as how we turned around a West Coast software development company that was neither brand-new nor 'captive.' As you know, the field of software development provides a home for brilliant technicians who would be uncomfortable under ordinary business conditions. Mention software companies to many insiders and they immediately visualize a big room in which hundreds of spacey, unmanageable hackers sit in a haze of pot smoke, stare into space, and occasionally write a few lines of code. There are such outfits, but our customer was not so picturesque, thank heaven. It was, however, a laid-back southern California company several years old with lots of promise that it hadn't fulfilled. It had good ideas for products, but it took too long to get them out.

"Like many other software companies, it had been organized from scratch through venture capital. Typically, such firms are fast on their feet during their initial operations because they're small, nimble, and have no communications problems. Short cycle times come naturally. Feedback is quick and effective. Everyone works extra hard because everyone has a piece of the action and expects big rewards within a few years. Accordingly, they thrive and grow. Then they inevitably have to restructure, departmentalize, compartmentalize, and standardize. Procedures and specifications are written up, short cycle time goes down the drain, and performance nosedives. That, in a nutshell, describes our customer's condition at the time we were hired.

"In this case, the company's investor group engaged us for nine months, during which we were to bring the firm out of the doldrums, install a capable CEO, and walk away. We accepted with the stipulation that for those nine months we would run the operation on a short-cycle-time basis. It was agreed. We also negotiated to work on a stock-incentive basis, because we could see that the software field was fertile ground indeed for Total Cycle Time and the entitlement payoffs would be substantial.

"Picture the surprised expressions on many faces when one of our representatives—a 20-year manufacturing type, not a hacker—arrived to run the company. That, however, was precisely what the situation called for, even though the company was white-collar wall to wall. Our acting CEO defined software development tasks at the outset and kept them from diverging from that single path. He eliminated steps that had no value-added content and managed work package sizes. I won't wear you out with the details, but the numbers are fresh in my mind. Within four months, the company was profitable again. Over nine months, the time for financial closing was cut from 40 days to 15. As barriers came down, product-development time dropped from a year to five months and utilized half the labor it had needed before: all in all 4.4 times more output per person. We used the cash we saved to double sales. We found a CEO who would institutionalize short cycle time and put the company on a 50 percent compound growth track. Now, that took place in an advanced white-collar environment with a full dose of Total Cycle Time culture change. It's a story that ought to make your R&D people think, and I'll use it on Tinker first chance I get.

"Experience has taught me that design and development people don't realize the tremendous handicaps they have to cope with in baseline situations, nor the liberation they'll enjoy once they eliminate those barriers. In R&D, barriers just get lost among the technical details, although they have nothing to do with them. And in big companies, the number of barriers can be colossal. I was astonished recently by what I saw when I visited a major Midwest auto parts supplier that constitutes a division of a Fortune 10 company. My host, who managed the R&D operation, believed it was performing near its entitlement. He talked me through a panoramic flow diagram depicting how a car's electrical system is developed. 'We think we have things under pretty tight control,' he told me. The cycle time was three years and eight months. Forty-four months! By the time their design entered production, some of its electronic components would be obsolete. And this in a business that is toe-to-toe with the Japanese!

"Just looking around, without doing an elaborate baseline study, I was sure the time could be cut in half. The company took us on strictly for that task, and inside of three months the cycle time had dropped to 30 months. By then, we had identified another year's worth of cycle time reduction that we're now coaching. Almost all of that was accomplished in generic areas, not design matters. Imagine what a difference that will make getting state-of-the-art cars onto the market."

King sipped the last of his coffee. The fire in the fireplace had gone to embers, and a waiter in knee breeches was snuffing the candles of a tin chandelier. Outside, the large, shiny Chrysler awaited. We rose to leave.

"I'm not the one who needs persuading," he said. "I've gone on record that I support you, and I'm gratified by our make/market progress. I'm not so confident, however, about similar miracles in R&D. I will say this, however: General Widget has got to cut its design and development time. The present rate will single-handedly kill the company off because we can't translate our good strategic ideas into products fast enough to exploit upcoming opportunities.

"Now I've given myself a case of financial jitters. Under the circumstances, you'd better take this," he said, handing me the check. "Good luck."

4

Momentum

I wasn't as worried as Victor King about reducing cycle time in General Widget's design/development loop. When I first talked with him by telephone, King had told me that General Widget's typical market window was eight years. Of the 96 months that elapsed from the time his company knew of a need until that need was exhausted, it was spending 30 months on product development alone. My analysis told me that it was possible to reduce time to market to 16 months, which would provide a 21 percent enlargement of the market window.

When I showed them the entitlement figures, King and Marketing VP Sellers were especially excited about three additional benefits. One had to do with price curves. By entering the market 14 months sooner, in the early stages of a product's life, General Widget could take advantage of prices that averaged 10 percent higher. The second advantage concerned customer service. By responding to demand in timely fashion, General Widget was likely to establish durable relationships with customers, which would mean repeat business. Third, cutting the development cycle time meant a commensurate reduction in development cost of more than 40 percent. All of this constituted an enormous opportunity: an eventual sales increase of $120 million, due to lengthened participation in the market window, with perhaps another $60 or $70 million due to average prices and market share if the product-development times were cut in half.

Obviously, speed and agility in the design/development loop was critical to such a strategy; so was the cooperation of key R&D personnel. King and Sellers had been believers from the start, but the skepticism of Dr. Witt Tinker, Research and Development VP, was also a matter of record. I suspected that his willingness to provide us with data was rooted in his conviction that such numbers would confirm that R&D was running at optimal speed.

The numbers, however, confirmed our estimates. Meanwhile, as has been seen, Tinker realized that shortening development cycle times would not be at the expense of creativity, but, more than any other senior manager in the company, he was committed to the principle of consensus. That meant that he would have to have the support of his R&D staff, and he frankly did not believe he was capable of overcoming the same sort of opposition among subordinates that he himself had once felt. As he told me, "There are a lot of senior people in R&D who have their own way of doing things, and a lot more individualists who just won't buy the idea. I'm pretty new to this company. If, after my initial reaction, I suddenly announce that I've converted to the gospel of Total Cycle Time, I'll look like a 90-day wonder. Maybe you guys should lead the charge. If you're successful, I'll throw my weight behind you."

Tinker was passing the Inspiration buck back to us. On the other hand, if his division was as full of tough-minded brains as he said, it was a cinch that its creativity would flourish once it was freed from red tape and delays. Perhaps the mentality was already in place, awaiting the right rationale. Tinker's people should also be able to grasp the principles of Total Cycle Time without the intensive training that was necessary in Manufacturing. Since we had no choice, we accepted the challenge and agreed to meet with all of Tinker's salaried research and development people, provided that at the Inspiration meeting Victor King be on hand to show the flag and throw his weight behind us.

The meeting was scheduled to take place in the same motor hotel we had used before. This time, I took the precaution of requesting three attendants for the coffee break. The meeting commenced on a day and time R&D customarily devoted to progress reviews. The difference was that this meeting would last two workdays, which gave it the air of importance we needed to convey. King agreed to show up for the opening formalities and return on day two to kick off general discussion. Another VIP unexpectedly showed up: marketing VP Sellers, who had invited himself to the R&D meeting.

On the appointed day of the R&D meeting, my teammates and I arrived early at the crack of dawn to make sure the coffee was hot and the overhead projector projected. Outside the door to the Betsy Ross Room, where we were scheduled to meet, I observed a floor stand adorned with press-in letters: "WELCOME GENERAL WIDGET DESIGN TEAM." Shades of Kaohsiung! I left it in place.

We figured that our audience had a high tolerance for detail and a longer than usual attention span. Accordingly, we hit with everything we had, running through a custom-tailored program that supplemented orientation remarks with a substantial dose of R&D data analysis, compressing the Inspiration, Identification, and Information phases into one session. We supplied a few carefully chosen anecdotes, including the California software story.

Throughout the session, Tinker acted as a master of ceremonies—no more, no less. He was scrupulously polite and positive, but quite self-effacing. And when King spoke, his remarks sounded a little canned. Like Tinker, he seemed to want us to bear the brunt of Inspiration.

Then Sellers unexpectedly came forward and asked to speak. Clipping the lapel microphone to his blazer and looking out over a crowd that clearly needed to be motivated, he was in his idiom: "Today, you R&D people have heard some persuasive arguments and seen more data than you ever wanted to. Much of what you have heard is sound, but theoretical. Some of what you have heard is sound, but philosophical. Some is plain common sense, verified by data. And it strikes me that Mr. King's remarks have been largely institutional.

"Now, while some of the ideas you've heard today might seem debatable—I myself have a problem with the correlation between short cycle time and high quality—nobody in his or her right mind would reject the overall principles. That would be like rejecting motherhood. Speaking for myself, and my division, I've bought into the concept and I'll deliver Marketing's share of the entitlement challenge. But it occurs to me that I see this matter of culture change from a perspective different from anyone else's in the room, which is why I'm here today. My perspective is not theoretical, philosophical, institutional, or strategic. My people are on the front lines. We can smell the gunpowder, we can smell possible defeat, and we are asking for support.

"Let's talk tactics. Let's talk survival—yours as well as ours. Out there on the front lines, we're getting clobbered by foreign competition. While we sit here getting used to new ideas, the Japanese and now the South Koreans are taking our markets. Total Cycle Time means General Widget can get its time to market down from 30 months to 16, which would be far superior to our Asian competitors.' You've seen a lot of figures showing the growth opportunity and cash hit that means for us. I'm here to ask if you've considered the alternative. If we stay at the 30-month time-to-market rate, we will not survive. On the other hand, if you people can design products faster, and if Manufacturing can turn them out likewise, I guarantee you Marketing can sell them. If there weren't a big market out there, our Pacific Basin competition would not have decided to build widgets.

"Getting back to the nitty-gritty: What does R&D stand to gain by shorter cycle times? More time to spend on outright research and development at the very least. What do you—we—have to lose if you don't make the change? Everything."

From the audience came a smattering of ingenuous applause. The atmosphere in the room had abruptly changed. Hands shot up, but Sellers, who had an instinct for dramatic effect, smiled, unclipped his mike, and made his way directly out of the room. It was our show again.

Besides energizing those who heard it, the Marketing VP's speech had flushed out Tinker, who was now excitedly polishing his glasses. As more hands shot up—perhaps a consensus?—Tinker stepped to the lectern and took the mike: "R&D will remove the logjams, eliminate the hurdles, and concentrate on what we all signed on to do. I trust you all can see now why I heartily endorse Total Cycle Time."

This was music to my ears. "Let's get all your questions answered," I said, "and see what we can do about beating the competition to market." It took a long time to field the questions and comments that were now buzzing around the room, but we knew the meeting had done the trick. Now to eliminate those logjams.

We had done enough homework to see where the major logjams were, although in ensuing months, R&D people proved adept at pinpointing others. It was clear that R&D had never operated in a relaxed fashion; quite the contrary. The need for speed, however, had exacerbated the cycle time problem, because R&D's research function was underweight. Its design effort, by the same token, was obese. Product development had been undertaken before the product in question was precisely defined. To make matters worse, software for production was under way before the complementary hardware was defined. The inevitable result had been a crunch of rework and redesign. Tinker's operation had 13 design efforts in progress. Those that were nearing completion were over budget and under pressure.

"I know Prince has the hots for these devices," Tinker told me on the day after the big meeting, "so I've restructured

R&D into task forces, and I've put my best people on the ones Prince wants the most."

"Wait a minute," I said. "Does that mean your senior people are assigned to the overdue designs?"

"Yes. Meanwhile, I'm trying to please Sellers in Marketing. I really wonder sometimes whether or not Marketing knows what it's doing. Six months ago, while we were killing ourselves on a design that was four months overdue, Marketing notified us to change the specs! The device had been one of Marketing's pet projects. It's not the first time that they've given us a fast shuffle after we've committed ourselves. In fact, rework was an old story when I arrived here five years ago. Reworking a key design usually involves new software, new custom devices from outside suppliers, reinventing the wheel. All this costs time and money, not to mention the resource overload."

"You've got problems," I said. "As you well know, the longer you take at the design stage, the more General Widget is edged out by fast-moving competitors. Sellers tells me that some of his spec changes are adjustments to late-breaking changes in the market. In other words, General Widget is hunting for the scraps left by companies with shorter time to market. What kind of talent do you have working on your beginning projects?"

"Well, since I've allocated my seasoned people to urgent matters, where greenhorns are of little use, I have my junior designers at work on new ones."

Tinker had made a major, but common, strategic error in the name of tactical expediency. "I think you've got your people assigned the wrong way round," I told him. "Putting inexperienced designers at the front end of a project almost predestines it to error and rework. It's asking too much of such people to expect them to hold their own against old pros like Sellers, whose hand is forced by shrinking windows of opportunity. Meanwhile, at the other end, your senior people wait to unscramble the inevitable accumulation of foul-ups. The conditions you're complaining about are self-perpetuating unless you reorganize."

Reorganize he did, only days after our discussion. Individual teams were created to concentrate on the development of a single product from conception through release to Manufacturing. Each team occupied a separate work area. The R&D drafting center was disbanded. Its people were assigned permanently to each team and physically located therein. The division's copying center was also disbanded and its people reassigned. Every team was now issued its own copying machine. Fax machines were installed between departments isolated in different buildings. They were soon getting a good workout.

The hero of the ensuing months turned out to be Tinker, who took up the banner and demonstrated real leadership. His most salutary step was to eliminate most of the formal, show-and-tell reviews by which he had kept tabs on various design groups. Instead, he made himself available to (and often went looking for) individuals and teams, searching out barriers to their progress. He thus focused his subordinates' creativity simultaneously upon both technical matters and cycle time reduction. Doing so eliminated the need for frequent group review sessions and simplified the preparation required. He stipulated that reviews should be shorter, more frequent, and without most of the accustomed show-and-tell.

One of R&D's biggest hang-ups had been the elaborate financial reporting system impartially imposed throughout General Widget. Tinker decided that what mattered was not the picayune detail of every step of every project, but how fast he could bring a project to completion. He therefore invited Prudence Cash to several design meetings, after which he asked that Finance come up with a simplified accounting procedure for R&D. Cash obliged. The new system, incidentally, reduced the number of signatures necessary for purchase orders from nine to two, which, trivial as it might seem, shaved more than two weeks off R&D's cycle time. Cash then persuaded Victor King to authorize the streamlining of approval levels throughout each division.

By the end of the first year, General Widget's design/development loop was not far behind make/market's in its move to entitlement. Furthermore, we knew from the record that Institutionalization would be easier in R&D than anywhere else in the company—except perhaps Kaohsiung. Institutionalization, the fifth I, was the home stretch for every division at General Widget.

5
Security

The fall and rise of orders in Marketing and the tortuous adjustments on the manufacturing line convinced me that Implementation was proceeding apace, but there was still much institutionalizing to be completed at the top level. Institutionalization could not occur until the company had a firm set of hierarchical measurements in place that were compatible with the new culture.

Total Cycle Time's measurements and controls are, of course, custom developed in each company. The ones devised for Manufacturing will illustrate the format and the process. We began by assembling Prince and his staff, including all of McMills's key people, in a large room equipped with an overhead projector. After explaining that we were there to set up a system of measurements, I called for suggestions. "Cycle time!" shouted one eager beaver, to accompanying applause. "Cycles of Learning!" shouted another. These were clearly what we wanted to hear, but there was a much deeper purpose here than checking that the fundamental lessons had been learned.

As each suggestion was made, I wrote it on a transparent slide so that it was projected on the wall. We soon had quite a few, including on-time delivery, rework percentage, first-pass yield, hours to recover, setup time, labor cost, labor content, and more. When the slide was covered with performance indices, I invited everyone to separate them into primary (fundamental and basic) and secondary (in support of a primary) categories.

We then put the primary indices onto a separate slide and after a few eliminations, rank-ordered them. We did the same with the secondary indices. About that time, someone suggested that the indices should vary from level to level within the organization. That led us to the top. We rank-ordered the indices that CEO King might properly concern himself with. We then proceeded to those important to Prince, then to those important to McMills, and so on. We then apportioned quantitative data accordingly throughout the hierarchy.

The process described above was repeated during subsequent weeks in Marketing, Research and Development, and Finance. As a result, the following set of hierarchical measurements was assembled for the company's top management:

Victor King (CEO)

- Customer service: percentage of on-time delivery
- Make/market cycle time
- Design/development cycle time
- Return on assets
- Visible inventory
- Invisible inventory
- Sales per person
- Total assets
- Total unit cost
- Sales
- Bookings

- Quality
- Cash

Haggard Prince (VP, Operations)
- Make/market cycle time
- Manufacturing cycle time
- Visible inventory
- Customer service
- Engineering-change-notice cycle time
- Purchasing cycle time
- Planning cycle time
- Unit cost
- Sales
- Linearity of sales

Butch McMills (Manager, Manufacturing)
- Manufacturing cycle time
- Work-in-process inventory
- Operator productivity
- Total manufacturing productivity
- Unit cost
- Equipment utilization
- Yield
- Rework
- Turnover

L. J. Byer (Manager, Purchasing)
- Vendor cycle time

- Raw material inventory
- Number of vendors
- Purchase price variance
- Purchasing cycle time

Eve Proctor or successor (Manager, Production Control)

- Sales and linearity of sales
- Inventory
- Percentage of on-time delivery
- Planning cycle time (part of make/market)
- Backlog
- Delinquencies

Hunter Merrit (Manager, Quality Control)

- Quality
- Customer returns
- Returns cycle time
- Percentage of on-time delivery

X. Pat Farr (Manager, General Widget Taiwan)

- Sales and linearity of sales
- Cycle time (part of make/market)
- Total unit cost
- Off-shore cost added
- Productivity of direct labor
- Productivity of plant
- Percentage of on-time delivery

- Inventory
- Total assets

Manny Bolster (Manager, Sustaining Engineering)

- Yield
- Rework
- Unit cost
- Engineering-change-notice cycle time

Moe Fixx (Manager, Equipment Maintenance)

- Mean time to repair
- 90 percent probability of hours to recover
- Equipment inventory, including spares
- Maintenance cost per unit
- Training level of work force

Hardy Sellers (VP, Marketing)

- Customer service: percentage of on-time delivery
- Bookings—linearity of bookings
- Customer returns
- Design/development cycle time (time to market)
- Make/market cycle time
- Finished goods and intermediate inventories

Mark Squiggle (Manager, Order Entry)

- Order-entry cycle time
- High-low ratio of cycle time

- Cost per order entered
- First-pass order-entry yield
- Linearity of order input
- Percentage of on-time delivery

Prudence Cash (VP, Finance)

- Cash
- Sales
- Profit
- Return on assets
- Spending
- Visible inventory
- Invisible inventory
- Balance sheet

Witt Tinker (VP, Research and Development)

- Design/development cycle time (time to market)
- First-pass design yield
- Performance to schedule
- Engineering change notices per design
- Cost per design
- Invisible inventory

King and his staff had been adding in these measurements and controls throughout the program. They would become the tools by which Total Cycle Time culture was institutionalized. Now the time had come to discard the old ones. This was an evolutionary process in which TGI's measurements were phased in, in addition to the traditional measurements. The new measurements became the framework for regularly scheduled monthly meetings between the CEO and his staff. In between the meetings, managers would submit a weekly, one-page "flash report" summary. The process that began at the top for Victor King was repeated for his subordinates, and for their subordinates, forming a pyramid of complementary, hierarchical measurements.

After a year and a half, the company was nearing its entitled performance. It was therefore appropriate to look back over the actual performance of the company when it had completed its latest fiscal year. At a management review meeting, we compared our original entitlement projections against General Widget's actual performance. The comparison is summarized in the table on page 132.

In sales and pretax profit, the company had come in on the money or slightly better than expected. Inventory results were substantially better than projected. Because fewer assets had been utilized, thanks largely to inventory reduction, the company had achieved higher sales and profit levels. The number of necessary blue-collar people was slightly higher than our original estimate for entitlement, but it was in line with the company's increase in sales. White-collar productivity had improved to a point where General Widget could function with 150 fewer employees, a result that exceeded our original expectation.

The company's make/market cycle time was better than our estimate by three workdays. Design/development, however, was still lagging behind expectations by two months, although Tinker was satisfied with the results. The overall criterion by which King measured results, however, was return on assets. In this category, General Widget had exceeded expectations, by about 1 percent overall. Generally speaking, performance was clearly within the ballpark of our expectations.

King wanted to know when and how we could ease ourselves out of the picture. "I think we should stick with General Widget for three more months via a monthly pulse," I told him. "We will monitor progress, act as coach and catalyst

GENERAL WIDGET COMPANY
RESULTS VERSUS ENTITLEMENT ESTIMATE
KEY MEASURES

	Beginning conditions	Actual results after two years	Entitlement	Difference
Sales	$600M	$762M	$750M	$12M
Pretax	30M	115M	112M	3M
Inventory	95M	72M	78M	6M
Total assets	$400M	$412M	$421M	$9M
Blue-collar people	3700	3900	3850	(50)
White-collar people	2800	2550	2700	150
Total	6500	6450	6550	100
Revenue per person	$92.3K	$118.1K	$114.5K	$ 3.6K
Make/market cycle time	110 days	42 days	45 days	3 days
Design/development cycle time	30 months	18 months	16 months	(2 months)
Return on assets	4.5%	16.7%	15.9%	0.8%

on new ideas, and make sure Institutionalization is truly happening. After that, we can almost reduce the pulse rate and let visitation drop to once a quarter.

"After a year of quarterly pulses, we can move to an annual physical examination, which will constitute a short-term assessment of your total operation. At that point, we will have become your silent partner, making sure your inventories as a percent of sales don't go up, making sure your pretax profit continues to improve, and making sure you have the proper strategy. We have specialists who are as enthralled by the prospects of maintaining your new culture as I've been about implementing it, and you'll get to know them well. We're prepared to continue those annual checkups for the foreseeable future—as long as it takes, in fact, to ensure that your organization has truly institutionalized Total Cycle Time culture. As you've seen, it can be very easy to revert to bad habits.

"Keep in mind, furthermore, that reaching entitlement is not a stopping point. Entitlement continually increases as your performance improves and as Cycles of Learning increase in frequency. In other words, nobody at General Widget should fixate on the entitlement figures we cited two years ago. Over the long haul, it's the culture that stays in place, not the numbers."

Sermons over Salads

For me, the high point of psychological payback comes not at the moment a company reaches entitlement, but when Total Cycle Time is irrefutably part of its culture. Only then do I unwind. At our second quarterly assessment, the news was all upbeat, so I felt I could relax, except for one thing. I was nagged by King's intermittent passiveness during the company's change of culture. Although his heart and mind were in the right place, I thought he relied too heavily upon corporate consensus and the mechanics of the system. I therefore needed to impress upon him one last time the absolute need for his attentive, firm enforcement of Total Cycle Time culture. It was time for one last night out with the CEO.

Somewhere near Valley Forge, under the stony gaze of a primitive colonial portrait, we munched salads served on pewter plates as big as pizzas. During a lull in the defoliation, I bore down hard on the need for forceful leadership at the top.

"General Widget has been through a drastic cultural change. All the mechanisms necessary to support that change are in place, but old habits die hard up and down the corporate line. Don't underestimate the force of habit, and don't tolerate for the sake of consensus any regression to those old habits. I'm talking particularly about your system of measurements and controls. It, and not your former criteria, has got to be the watchword from now on. And you, as CEO, must be a very visible presence in enforcing that system until it is second nature."

"I understand what you're saying and why you're saying it," said King. "There have been times over the last months when I might have been more of a sparkplug. At first, I wasn't sure I agreed with your dictum about top-down enforcement because I thought it was counterproductive. I figured if Total Cycle Time was as sensible as you said, it ought to take root at General Widget without a lot of uncharacteristic arm twisting. I was especially worried about resistance in R&D. But at the same time, I wasn't completely sure our R&D could be won over by any means. Call it a crisis of faith. I didn't want that to show, so, like Tinker, I did little more than go through the motions. But that was a long time ago. Read my lips: General Widget will suffer no relapse. But tell me, does Total Cycle Time ever get to be second nature, as you said?"

"Sure," I answered, "but getting there is partly a matter of strong and continued top-down pressure. I wish we'd had this conversation earlier; I'd have told you about the mea-

sures I had to take to institutionalize Total Cycle Time at
RCA's Findlay, Ohio, factory."

"I have a feeling you're going to tell me now."

"Well, since you insist....The incident took place during
my days as an RCA executive. That plant was one of several
that reported to me, and it was my best candidate for Total
Cycle Time. It had been running comfortably, without
change, for 20 years. It needed to change. It was a long way
from RCA headquarters; in fact, it was a long way from any
other semiconductor plant, so it looked to me like a green-
house where cultural change might be cultivated without distraction.

"We worked wonders at Findlay, but it wasn't easy at first.
The first task was to dramatize that things were going to
change, and to do so, I resorted to tactics that I know are not
your style. But they worked. For example, on my first day at
Findlay, touring the grounds, I noticed that many of the
parking places in the company lot were reserved for management. I despise things like that; they bring out the worst in
everybody. 'You see those signs?' I asked the plant manager.
He did. 'It's nine-thirty. By noon those signs are to be
painted over. No more personalized parking spots.' By noon
the signs had disappeared. When I walked through the plant,
I noticed an obstructive wall partition. 'That wall has to come
down right away,' I said. 'Two days from now, I'll need a
photograph of this area, and the partition must be gone.' My
subordinates said they didn't understand. 'You don't have
to,' I told them, 'but you do need to understand that when a
change is specified it needs to be completed very quickly.' Of
course, I did have a valid reason to remove the wall, but at
the time, making a point that there was a new 'broom' that
was about to do some sweeping seemed more important than
a lengthy justification. That could come later. In the mean-
time, the Findlay people knew they'd better prepare for a
substantial change in culture.

"We had a lot of work to do there, and I believe those first
authoritative commands saved me a lot of time. We reduced

the plant's cycle time from 45 days to 10 days, and in the bargain we institutionalized the culture. It stuck. Today, Findlay still operates on a 10-day cycle time, even though its production tasks are far more demanding.

"General Widget is long past the point when melodramatic demonstrations are called for," I continued, "unless, somehow, your measurements and controls prove inadequate. I was reeducated to just this point a few months back. My company had undertaken an incentive-based contract to improve order-entry cycle time for a major U.S. company. We did very well, and when we sent in our bill the client canceled the program because the incentive payment was too large! We, of course, protested. The client told us that its financial reporting mechanisms, which were quite conventional, provided no way to quantify the gains made through Total Cycle Time against the costs incurred during the process. The costs—our incentive fee—showed on the profit statement; the benefits did not, at least as an item. Consequently, the individual manager who had had the foresight to undertake the program, and whose operation was obviously making impressive headway, actually looked bad on the corporate financial review. End of program. Frustrating, eh?

"On the other hand, I've had a gratifying experience with a company of my own, B & B Electromatic. B & B is a small manufacturing firm; Butch McMills can tell you all about it sometime. It's had its problems, but when things started to improve, I awarded an annual bonus in recognition of the improvement. Then it occurred to me that a plain old bonus did not fit my concepts of cycle time. Employees could not relate it to specific causes because the award covered a whole year. Aside from morale boosting, the bonus wasn't having an impact on their work. In 1988, I switched to a system that utilized Cycles of Learning and feedback loops. The new system uses a monthly point index. Everyone in the company, from the president to the janitor, participates. The monthly point index ranges from 0 to 20—it can also go negative— and is tied to operating profit. Everyone knows how many dollars she or he receives per point and thus can track the bonus system month by month. Its immediate impact was that the company's performance improved still further: Cycle times shortened, inventories dropped, customer response speeded up, and overtime and absenteeism disappeared. I count all this as a neat merger of proper measurements and controls with the benefits of Cycles of Learning. And, to a person, B & B's work force understands and is actively involved in the company's new culture. Once Total Cycle Time is institutionalized, any vigilant management team will see opportunities like that to refine its system. Watch for them."

That was enough of a sermon. King's assurances had let me relax at last. It was time to let him do a little crowing. "The figures your people have been giving us look terrific," I said. "What's the scuttlebutt?"

"It's better than it looks," said King. "I met with our marketing people yesterday. Hardy Sellers is walking on air because we're taking market share from our competitors. How sweet it is! Sellers tells me General Widget's quality and customer service is still winning us contracts in areas where the Japanese had the business all to themselves. Hunter Meritt, who had been licking his wounds ever since he was made quality manager, and who was developing an inferiority complex into the bargain, is now, of course, a hero. He has no intention of resting on his laurels at this point, and with the kind of feedback he's getting, he shouldn't have to.

"As you know, we now expect to finish first in the race for the new, lightweight, all-weather Widgeroo. When that item hits the market, we'll be leading the whole industry into a new era of growth. Tinker and the rest of R&D are already at work on another potential world-beater, the Widgerino. As an old widgeteer, I was beginning to think of myself as an endangered species, so I don't have to tell you how much all this tickles me. Well, I *can* tell you. For the first time in three years, I'm going fishing without a portable telephone in my tackle box.

"Hmmm....I think I'll have the trout tonight."

6

Reflection

Fishing was an interest I shared with Victor King. I do most of mine in Louisiana, at a getaway home I retreat to every chance I get. The house is built on land which included a rain-washed gully that, over the years, I reshaped into a well-stocked lake. The setting is relaxing, secluded, and gently scenic. Fishing that lake, I have found, serves two salutary purposes. The chore is simple enough to allow me to think over problems in a fresh setting; or, depending on my mood and the hypnotic effect of ripples on the surface, engrossing enough to provide some therapeutic escape from business pressures. I enjoy the spot so much that an occasional strike seems like a real bonus. Lately, I took a six-pound bass I had caught there to a taxidermist. It now hangs on the wall of my office overlooking the lake, as an encouragement for guests to do some fishing with me.

Victor King, I found out, approached his hobby a bit more seriously. He had a lodge-style summer home on expansive Lake Wallenpaupack in the Poconos, the kind of house that comes equipped with a fieldstone fireplace and sets of mounted antlers in the living room. King himself had a closet full of smart fishing togs and a bass boat tied up at his dock that, he said, could skim around the lake "quite quickly."

(That, I learned, was a considerable understatement.) Victor King does not stuff his fish; he eats them.

All of which I found out several months after I had concluded my last monthly visit to General Widget and accepted an invitation from King to join him at his getaway home. I had a feeling I was in for the kind of weekend where fishing is a backdrop for serious business talk. I was right, although the talk was not altogether serious.

When I arrived on a sunny spring afternoon, King was in a good mood, dressed for the water, and eager to bring me up to date on recent events in Philadelphia. I changed clothes, selected a graphite rod from his impressive collection, and joined him at lakeside. After a fast ride to King's preferred spot, ensconced in the swivel seats of the "Widgeroo," we cast our lines.

"I've always been a believer in the ability of talented people to rise to any occasion," King began. "I guess that's why part of your attitude about Total Cycle Time bothered me at first. When you insisted that 'cultures, not people are the problem,' you struck me as a technocrat who lacked sensitivity for the special abilities of individuals, as though anybody could become a cog in the wheels of your preconceived system. Being a consensus-based manager who listens to the misgivings of my subordinates, I totally missed your point that General Widget's problems were a function of culture, not individual shortcomings. In other words, I was filtering your message through my own cultural bias."

"That's one of the reasons why it usually takes outsiders to oversee effective cultural change," I answered. "But now that you have some hindsight, how have your managers been coping?"

"It's surprising, even to me," said King. "They're doing fine. When I first told you we had good people in the company, I realized I was making a generalization, and perhaps a sentimental one at that. I had privately concluded that our people were good but not great—no champs—and that we would almost certainly have to do some house cleaning. But every top manager, from the early believers through the kickers and screamers, is comfortable with Total Cycle Time: no departures, no terminations. From where I sit, one of the best results has been the decrease in office politics and back-biting. Marketing has quit beating up on Manufacturing, Manufacturing has taken the chip off its shoulder, R&D people no longer play the role of long-suffering geniuses, line people don't complain about the burdens inflicted on them by Corporate....You guys cost us a lot, but I realize you really earned it and we ended up with at least a ten-to-one return on the cost. Yet, if it weren't for all the sweat we put into reaching entitlement, I would still think we got off easy. Was it luck? Hard work? Inevitability?"

"Some of each," I replied, "although not in equal weights. General Widget's problem was never one of managerial dedication—you told me that during our first conversation. The fact is, your subordinates are now enjoying what you yourself noticed fairly early: that short-cycle-time culture gives a manager more time to think creatively about what matters most and also provides him or her better tools to manage with. Any qualified executive's morale and creativity will improve in such an environment."

I had read that the company's improved position had made it an attractive investment prospect, and I asked King about that. He brushed the matter aside: "We attracted the attention of Unigadget two months back. They were trying to diversify and had picked up Western Widget for a song, but lately our stock had become too pricey for a merger or take-over. On the other hand, we've made some interesting moves. We're keeping the Kaohsiung operation, which is going great guns in its new role of competing in the Pacific Rim market. But we've decided to do a little vertical integration of our own closer to home. Have you ever heard of Gizmolab? It's a little company near us in Bridesburg that produces the alabaster implants we use. It's a good vendor, no supply problems or anything like that. But we're going to be needing a lot more implants, some of them custom, so I went over there a couple of months ago to check things out. Living with TGI has given me a sharp eye for cycle times, and I'm sure there's room for improvement at Gizmolab. I'm also sure General Widget could turn that operation around. Meanwhile, however, we're negotiating to acquire Newidget, whose cycle times are horrendous. Talk about opportunity! If that goes through, I think I can get the board to buy Gizmolab. Then we'll combine Newidget and Gizmolab into a separate subsidiary under Prince. I figure Sellers can handle Philadelphia. By the way, Fred Slack wants to sell Amalgamated Doodad to us, but we're not quite ready for that. Whoa! I've got a strike!"

King insisted on cleaning the fish we were to have for dinner, which was okay with me. When the meal was over, he told me he had gotten a letter from an old Wharton School buddy whose company was having problems with market share and cash flow. "The company's name is Southern Wotnot, in Atlanta. Lately they've changed their name to Sowonot, but the new name hides a multitude of problems. My friend, Larry Flapp, is CEO. The problems he described sounded familiar," King said. "You'd recognize them in a flash, and I know just what you'd say. Well, I haven't had much time lately, and I don't know much about Larry's business, so I wrote out a list of pointers he could use to check for long cycle time. I think it's great. You might find it a useful troubleshooting device."

"Sure," I replied. "Do you have a copy?"

"Not so fast. It's not a giveaway. It'll cost you a weekend of fishing in Louisiana."

CHECKLIST FOR A FRIEND

Larry—These are the symptoms of long cycle time.

MAKE/MARKET

___ Are you faced with many missed schedules and customer complaints?

___ Are your deliveries within one or two days of the promised date
less than 90 percent of the time?

___ Do your delinquencies to customers run longer than a week?

___ Are you resistant to customers' requests for schedule changes?

___ In Manufacturing, is there a high level of expediting or hot lots?

___ Do your manufacturing change notices take too long?

___ Is there nonlinearity in your order input and sales output (more
than 35 percent in the last week of the month)?

___ Are your inventory levels above 15 percent of sales?

___ Are there many hold files at Order Entry?

___ Is your product quality average? Is it below average?

___ Are your first-pass yields below 95 percent?

___ Is your productivity equal to your competition's?

___ Is your rework level high?

___ Is your employee morale declining?

___ Is there a high degree of employee turnover?

DESIGN/DEVELOPMENT

___ Are your products usually late to market?

___ Is your reliance upon old products increasing?

___ Are your designers frustrated?

___ Are your marketing people frustrated?

I hope this list is of some help, and trust that you can say no
to most of these items!

In haste,
Victor

I decided that Victor's checklist was worth putting in a book.
King got his weekend in Louisiana, and I even cleaned what
he caught. When the fishing was over and I returned to
headquarters, there was a message waiting on my terminal:
Larry Flapp had called from Atlanta and wanted to talk.

7
Opportunity

Although the General Widget story highlights the theory and application of Total Cycle Time, a few vital and interesting points remain to be made about the dynamics of the system and its impact on competitiveness.

As said in Chapter 1, competitiveness consists of three R's: responsiveness to customers' needs, results acceleration, and resource effectiveness. Total Cycle Time acts upon and interlocks these three elements with powerful results.

Most businesses today acknowledge that what differentiates them most from their competitors is customer responsiveness. If they provide customers with the desired quality products in the desired mix and quantity and do so in a timely and cost-effective fashion, they will gain market share. Most likely, they will also build a growing, symbiotic relationship with each satisfied customer.

The cycle of customer service dominates the make/market loop of every business. In today's world, responsiveness is more and more a matter of delivering an ever-changing product mix within an ever-shrinking time span. Performance that falls short of that will fail.

Too many companies, using the wrong indices of measurement, convince themselves that their customer service is optimal, yet they regularly miss delivery deadlines, deliver in the wrong mix, fight changes in a customer's order, or hold up the debut of a new product because they are unable to develop a component for it on schedule. Unlike the leader at General Widget, who saw the writing on the wall, too many management teams accept such glitches as part of the headaches of doing business and devote a great deal of time to coping with them. In other words, they take such headaches in stride. They should not. It requires scant imagination to see how shortened cycle times will remove major obstacles to better customer service. And the payoffs are gratifying.

The impact of short cycle time on customer responsiveness may be seen from Thomas Group's accumulated experience: In manufacturing-based businesses, a 50 percent reduction in the make/market loop's customer service cycle time—a typical result—can increase market share by 5 to 10 percent with the same products.

Now to the second component of competitiveness: the acceleration of results. The answer here is to creatively exploit Cycles of Learning to enhance future performance. Throughout the previous chapters, the point was repeatedly made that Total Cycle Time is the driver of competitiveness and quality. All the improvements that pushed General Widget from baseline to entitlement (and which will work for any other company as well) were themselves driven by Cycles of Learning.

The discovery of Cycles of Learning dates back to my days at Texas Instruments in the 1960s, when it became clear that a formal feedback loop was absolutely essential if the lessons of experience were to be exploited creatively. Then, having built the requisite creative and management forcing functions into the feedback loops, I was able to fine-tune some important but overgeneralized business assumptions.

At the time, TI was enamored of the Boston Consulting Groups' now-famous learning-curve/market-share theory [the gist of which may be found in that group's publication, *Perspectives on Experience* (Boston: Boston Consulting

Group, 1968)]. Learning-curve thinking became almost a religion at TI and at many other fast-paced, highly competitive companies. According to the theory, cost drops by a predictable percentage whenever cumulative volume doubles. The downward slope of costs and prices, known as the learning curve, occurs because efficiency increases with experience and volume. Assuming that relative cost determines a company's market share, strategists can plot future points at which their costs and prices will drop, and they can plan accordingly. For example, if the millionth unit of a product costs one dollar, and if the learning curve's projected slope is 70 percent, the two-millionth unit is expected to cost 70 cents. Learning-curve theory was supposed to take some of the guesswork out of competing for market share.

But, as I came to understand, there are two kinds of learning, and the proportion of each determines the steepness of a learning curve. One, which involves gradual, repetitive improvement of skills and long-term dilution of fixed costs, is largely volume-related: Do something long enough and you get speedy at it. The second type of learning is creativity-related, an important insight that occurs during a single Cycle of Learning. The impact of breakthroughs is quick and dramatic. Breakthroughs therefore constitute step functions on a learning curve and can sharply steepen its slope. More Cycles of Learning mean more breakthroughs.

Creative breakthroughs improve the chances of higher first-pass yield. As cycle times are reduced, first-pass yields increase because Cycles of Learning generate creative thought and more rapid feedback, provided that a structured feedback loop, complete with a management forcing function, is established.

The following discovery, which came during an accelerating series of Cycles of Learning, exemplifies a creative breakthrough. It is very important. The slope of a learning curve is more dependent upon Cycles of Learning than cumulative volume. In complex processes, doubling the Cycles of Learning can steepen a learning curve by 10 percent. Shorter cycle

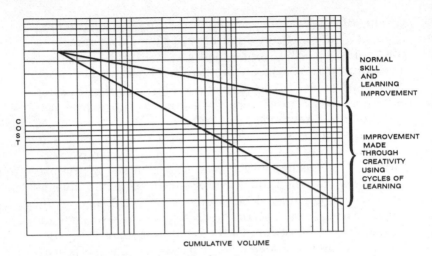

The two kinds of learning in the learning curve.

times mean more Cycles of Learning. More Cycles of Learning mean more creative breakthroughs. A small, agile company exploiting its Cycles of Learning can outperform a high-volume, slow-moving giant.

The third component of competitiveness is the effective use of resources. General Widget's story dramatized how shortening cycle times can reduce inventory, liberate cash, and reduce waste—improvements that require no further elaboration here. Similar dramatic advances, however, can be realized in the productivity of people.

As a company's culture shifts from long to short cycle time, the impact on blue-collar and white-collar employees is tremendous. At first, this phenomenon can be downright upsetting, because the comfort of doing things the familiar way has evaporated and people feel threatened.

The problem is especially acute in a blue-collar manufacturing context. There, long cycle times have bred high inventory levels, the ostensible purpose of which is to insure against unexpected disruptions in production. In such an environment, inventory also serves the psychological function of assuring people that they will not run out of work or miss a schedule. Typically, a production line's inventory is two or three times the amount necessary in short-cycle-time conditions. As it starts to disappear, people can get decidedly edgy. Another source of jitters is the frequent misunderstanding of short cycle time. Many line supervisors are wary because they reflexively fear that reducing inventory will require a commensurate increase in labor and equipment. The principle that less in means more out just does not make sense to such people. For their part, many line workers can't accept the fact that the changes will remove barriers to efficiency, allowing them to increase productivity without increasing their pace. Too often, their first impression is that they will have to speed up. It is absolutely essential that the truth of the matter be clarified, repeatedly, to offset anxieties. Anxieties also grow because, as cycle times drop and previously unseen barriers are exposed, incompetence reveals itself.

After a while, however, drooping morale inevitably revives and starts to climb, usually to a point higher than under the old culture. That is because, with inventories balanced and obstructions eliminated, people no longer have to endure adverse wait stoppages or interruptions. They are now free to perform quality work and get the feedback that confirms it.

In the long run, moving to entitlement is a liberating experience. By way of example: We recently examined a production line bogged down by inspection requirements whose justification was quality control. A product moved back and forth between two departments where value was added. As each item left department A, it was carefully cleaned, inspected, and shipped to department B. Immediately upon its arrival at B, the item received another identical cleaning and inspection. After it was processed, B again cleaned and inspected it, then routed it promptly back to A, where—you guessed it. All that redundant inspection and cleaning was both a cause and effect of long cycle times, but at the time we arrived, the unquestioning company, hoping to raise productivity by cutting labor content, was about to *automate* the inspection steps! The solution, of course, was to reduce the production cycle time, simultaneously improving quality and eliminating the need for all but a final inspection.

It is amazing how many business processes that grew like Topsy are earnestly perpetuated and even expanded by inattentive management. Simplifying such processes is part of any move to entitlement, so here is a figure that should get a few to pay attention: Typically, companies with a Total Cycle Time culture achieve productivity increases of about 20 percent in blue-collar areas.

The issue of white-collar productivity is one that has escaped the intense scrutiny that industrial engineers, psychologists, efficiency experts, and assorted consultants have lavished on direct labor. It is therefore no surprise that white-collar sectors offer the greatest potential for improvement. Years of rude awakenings have taught me that white-collar people are generally at work on ill-conceived, resource-hungry processes that have low first-pass yields and too small a value-added content. The farther they are from the manufacturing floor, the worse these conditions are.

Some types of low-level white-collar productivity have to be seen to be believed. Many companies have created labyrinthine check-and-balance processes because of the risks associated with long cycle times. In one case, we discovered that a client's order-entry cycle cross-checked the same data at least six times. The reason for the repetition was that an order in process had to wait here and there for action. Each time processing was resumed, the procedure was to recheck the data in case some error had crept in. By reducing cycle time by 5 to 1, which lowered the error rate, all but one of these checks could be eliminated. In another situation, we encountered an internal organization of more than 50 people devoted purely to unscrambling errors made during order entry. Shortening cycle time and using the resulting Cycles of Learning reduced the staff to five. Those people could now work strictly as monitors, and thus they improved their own productivity 15 times over.

Take another white-collar area: sales. In a long-cycle-time environment, salespeople commonly spend 30 percent or more of their time tracking and checking on orders for their customers. The longer the cycle time, the less predictable the delivery dates. Because customers typically cannot live with imprecise delivery dates, the burden of expediting falls on the person who has made the sale. The requisite corresponding and calling costs money and subtracts from outright sales effort and positive customer service. Short cycle times can free up 20 to 30 percent of a salesperson's time. In a sales force of a 100, that's equivalent to adding 20 or 30 new people *at no cost.*

Among managers, short cycle time must often combat a powerfully obstructive mind-set. Managers usually possess hefty egos, a track record that the company deems successful, and a resistance to any implication that their priorities may be out of whack. Characteristically, they base their performance indices on the past, trying to accomplish incremental improvements over time. They often "manage" problems of long cycle time through excessive reviews, procedures, controls, inventory, and inspections, tactics that cost time and money but add no value. Often captives of the business school concept of management by exception, they concentrate on trouble spots instead of analyzing and improving things that are going right. Even quality-improvement teams usually act as fire fighters, hosing down problems here and there.

The goal for management should be to concentrate on upgrading the 95 percent that is going right without neglecting the subpar 5 percent. That is a prerequisite for Total Cycle Time, in which it is the manager's responsibility to adopt measurements and controls to insure proper use of increased Cycles of Learning and to institutionalize short-cycle-time results.

There are other types of resistance to the new culture. Just as line workers draw comfort from stacks of inventory assuring them there is work to do, managers draw comfort from

piles of paper requiring their attention. Getting through half
a pile of paper in a day—a cycle time of two days—assures
managers that there will be a lot for them and their subordinates to do tomorrow. Taking their cues from the boss, subordinates will make that work last or, matching the boss's
speed, will build a backlog.

Work will also last if it is held up by a manager's habit of
postponing important decisions until Monday morning,
when he or she is fresh, or by the endless review meetings
that accompany long cycle time, or by leisurely internal mail
cycles. How can it take longer to route an interoffice memo
than to send it across a continent? Why should it? How many
days does such a circumstance add to every white-collar cycle? And when a manager is away from the office for days or
weeks, why is so little effort made to cover that gap? No one
would tolerate such a vacancy on a manufacturing line.

Even when the merits of Total Cycle Time are accepted in
principle, winning white-collar hearts and minds is difficult
in the early stages because the push to entitlement constitutes
a surcharge on managerial time. Short-cycle-time culture is
not a "program," so it cannot be spearheaded by staff or spe-
cially designated "champions." The buck stops at the desks of
in-place managers. There is thus no way to sugarcoat the fact
that longer hours are involved. Soon, however, the surcharge
diminishes to zero. Soon afterward, each manager discovers
a net gain in discretionary time as business becomes predictable, customer complaints subside, and time once spent in
progress reviews can be brought to bear elsewhere. In other
words, managers gain time in which to think. Employees can
see a difference, too, and eventually the new culture wins
consensus. I should emphasize at this point that almost everyone involved in a move to entitlement, from the top
down, is capable of successfully undergoing such rites of pas-
sage. Any manager worth his or her salt will get downright
excited about the new regime once a few of its impacts are
perceived. Any employee will do likewise once the measurements, controls, and performance criteria are in place.

But they will not get excited immediately. At first, Implementation can look uncongenial to managers and other white-collar types who are comfortable inside the cocoon of the old system. The problem is fundamentally the same as in a blue-collar context: High work inventories symbolize job security. As cycle times and inventory levels go down, however, the feeling of security drops commensurately. Expressed diagramatically, employees' "comfort curves" drop sharply early in the Implementation stage. Usually, those most discomfited are those who are least competent. But as Total Cycle Time progresses and performance improvements are perceived, comfort curves rise steadily to a point higher than under the old regime.

The bottom line for white-collar productivity improvement can be astounding. Because there is so much room for improvement, and because, thanks to its apparent benefits, white-collar people inevitably adopt Total Cycle Time culture, productivity increases of 20 percent are quite common. Increases of 100 percent are by no means unusual.

The ability to endure the discomfiture of phases of Imple-

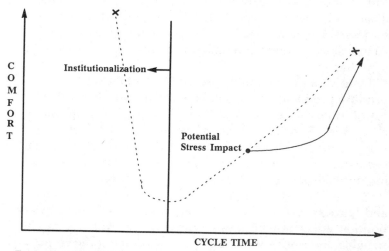

Typical comfort curve.

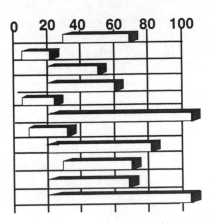

TOTAL CYCLE TIME
REVENUES
INVENTORIES
INVISIBLE INVENTORIES
BLUE–COLLAR PRODUCTIVITY
WHITE–COLLAR PRODUCTIVITY
DEPRECIATION
SCRAP
DELIVERY LEAD TIMES
TIME–TO–MARKET
RETURN ON ASSETS

Ranges of Improvement.

mentation until comfort curves turn upward is almost universal among American businesspeople. I attribute this happy circumstance to national values. Unlike workers in some other cultures, Americans are pragmatic enough to accept a new concept that promises dramatic results, and to live with temporary discomfort for long-range improvement. That is why, when Total Cycle Time is applied to American business, people are seldom the problem. That is also why Americans are uniquely qualified to fully exploit such salutary change.

Think of it: The changes wrought by Total Cycle Time can produce productivity gains in blue-collar and white-collar areas of 10 to 20 percent and 20 to 100 percent, respectively, along with 5 to 20 percent gains in the use of plant and equipment. The new culture can produce a 30 to 70 percent reduction in time to market, with sales increases from resulting market-share gains between 5 and 50 percent.

Matched with the benefits of sound inventory management and controls that monitor true total costs, those unique assets position American businesses perfectly to win the urgent struggle for worldwide competitiveness. The time to act is now, and the tool is Total Cycle Time.

Glossary

Baseline: The accustomed, everyday performance level of a business.

Comfort Curve: The index of psychological security within a business, which tends to be high in familiar circumstances, declines as cycle times are systematically reduced, and climbs again as short-cycle-time culture is institutionalized.

Cycle of Learning: The opportunity to improve performance that occurs when the lessons of experience are systematically exploited. Cycles of Learning are computed by dividing the number of workdays in a year during a single process by the process cycle time expressed in days.

Cycle Time: The elapsed time between the commencement and completion of a task. In manufacturing, it is calculated as the number of units of work-in-process inventory divided by the number of units processed in a specific period.

Design/Development Loop: A major business cycle encompassing all steps in the development of new products or services, beginning with the identification of market need and ending with the capability of cost-effective production.

Entitlement: The optimum performance level attainable by a business using its existing resources.

Feedback Loop: A structured procedure, including a management forcing function, by which the lessons of a Cycle of Learning are creatively exploited.

First-Pass Yield: The measure of products or services that are acceptably completed on the first attempt without requiring remedial action or rework.

Five I's: The components of the roadmap for culture change within a company. (*See* Inspiration, Identification, Information, Implementation, Institutionalization.)

High-Low Diagnostics: An analytical technique for performance evaluation in which best- and worst-case data are scrutinized to reveal the barriers to improved productivity.

Identification: The second phase of Total Cycle Time's culture change, in which the components for improving performance are pinpointed. One of the Five I's of the culture change roadmap.

Implementation: The phase of culture change in which problems are solved and existing resources are redeployed to achieve entitlement. Implementation begins early and continues throughout the movement from baseline to entitlement. One of the Five I's of the culture change roadmap.

Information: A phase of corporate culture change in which employees are trained in the necessary skills to move from baseline to entitlement. One of the Five I's of the culture change roadmap.

Inspiration: The first phase of a company's move from baseline to entitlement, in which the need for culture change is expressed and embraced. One of the Five I's of the culture change roadmap.

Institutionalization: The last phase of a company's move from baseline to entitlement, in which implemented changes are in place and become second nature within the organization, completing the process of culture change. The imposition of accurate measurements and controls are integral to this process. One of the Five I's of the culture change roadmap.

Invisible Inventory: Value within a company which is not itemized in conventional accounting procedures. Examples include new designs in process, cost-reduction programs in process, and receivables in process. Invisible inventory is calculated by multiplying the spending rate by the cycle time to visible result.

Make/Market Loop: A major business cycle encompassing all activities of manufacturing and sales, from the quotation of prices to a customer through the collection of receivables.

Strategic Thrust Loop: A major business cycle encompassing all activities in a company's long-range planning function, from the identification of an opportunity through its establishment as a normal sector of a company's business.

Theoretical Cycle Time: The back-to-back process time required for a single unit to complete all stages of a task without waiting, stoppage, or time lost due to error.

Three R's: The components of competitiveness: responsiveness to customers' needs, results acceleration, and resource effectiveness.

Total Product Cost: A measurement that accurately reflects the cost of a product, computed by dividing the sales level less pretax profit by the number of units shipped.

Visible Inventory: The accounting-based inventory within a company, including raw material, work in process, and finished goods on hand.

Index

About the Author

PHILIP R. THOMAS is founder and chairman of the board of Thomas Group, Inc., Irving, Texas. During his 20 years as an executive at Texas Instruments, General Instruments, Fairchild, and RCA, Thomas proved the methodology of Total Cycle Time, significantly improving the competitiveness of the businesses he managed, despite differences in corporate culture and geographic location. Since 1978, he has successfully introduced his system to improve corporate competitiveness and streamline operational and new product cycle times at companies ranging from Fortune 10 firms to entrepreneurial start-ups, from high-tech manufacturing-based industries to heavy manufacturing to software companies.

KENNETH R. MARTIN is the author or coauthor of a number of books on business and maritime history. He lives in Woolwich, Maine.